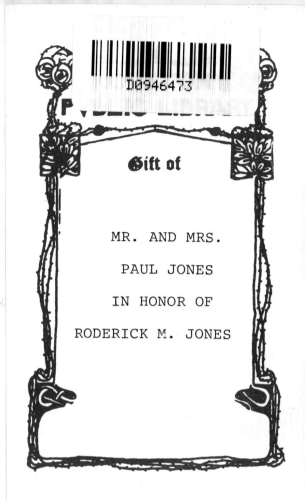

ANGLO-SAXON TOWERS

An Architectural and Historical Study

ANGLO-SAXON TOWERS

An Architectural and Historical Study

by

E. A. FISHER, MA, DSc

AUGUSTUS M. KELLEY PUBLISHERS

New York

© E. A. Fisher 1969

Published in the United States of America
by Augustus M. Kelley Publishers
New York 1969
76-77876

Printed in Great Britain
by Clarke Doble & Brendon Limited Plymouth

Contents

	Page
List of illustrations	7
Preface	9

PART I   INTRODUCTION TO ANGLO-SAXON TOWERS   15

Centrally-planned churches   16
Fortified or defence towers   22
Bell towers   22
Staircase towers   25
Pylons   26

PART II   TOWERS IN SAXON ENGLAND   29

1   *Central towers*   29
    Centrally-planned churches
    Quoining
    Turriform churches
    Cruciform churches

2   *Bell towers*   49
    Porch towers
    English Carolingian towers
    Lincolnshire bell towers
    Axial towers
    Western annexes to western towers
    Staircase towers
    Adjuncts to western towers

3   *Round towers*   70
    East Anglian round towers
    Irish round towers

4   *Other towers and their uses*   85
    Fortified or defence towers
    Dimensions of western towers
    Some other ecclesiological uses of towers

		Page
5	*Belfries*	95
	Belfry openings	
	Mid-wall columns and bulging balusters	
	Capitals and bases in belfry openings	
	Openings in ground floors	
	Circular openings or occuli	
	Other types of openings	
	Horse-shoe arches	
	Unexplained openings in towers	
6	*Pilaster strip-work*	116
	On walls (Lombard bands and blind arcading)	
	Strip-work around openings	
	'Soffit roll system' of ornamentation	
	German blind arcading	
	Early history of pilaster strip-work	
	Armenian art and culture and their influence in Western Europe	

PART III   GAZETTEER | | 137

Location of Saxon towers	137
Saxon towers and their main architectural features	148
Notes	185
Bibliography	193
Acknowledgments	197
Index of persons	199
Index of places and sites	200
General and Architectural Index	206

List of Illustrations

PLATES

	Page
Irish round tower	17
Bishopstone, Sussex	17
Bywell, St Andrew's tower	18
Skipwith tower	18
Jarrow, tower belfries	35
Barton-on-Humber tower	35
Skipwith, tower arch	36
Canterbury, St Mildred's nave	36
Barton-on-Humber tower	36
Barton-on-Humber, doorway	36
Haddiscoe tower	53
Roughton tower	53
Bolam, belfry opening	54
Brigstock, window and quoin	54
Monkwearmouth, balusters	54
Deerhurst, tower openings	54
Stow, crossing arch	71
Sompting tower arch	71
Haddiscoe tower arch	71
Breamore, arch to porticus	71
St Peter-at-Gowts tower	72
St Mary-at-Coslany tower	72
Brixworth tower	89
Barnack tower	89
Earls Barton tower	90
Earls Barton, banded balusters	90
Barnack, tower arch	90
Cambridge, St Benet's	90
Haddiscoe, belfry opening	107
Brixworth, triple opening	107
Colchester, Holy Trinity	107
Bosham, nave wall	107

		Page
Deerhurst, gable-headed double opening		108
Monkwearmouth, tower		108
Wickham tower		133
Clapham tower		133
Sompting tower, from north		134
Sompting tower, from south		134
Bosham tower		135
Little Bardfield tower		135
Breamore tower		136
Oxford, St Michael's		136

FIGURES IN TEXT

1	St Riquier plan	20
2	St Riquier before AD 1090	21
3	Aachen, Charlemagne's Palace Chapel plan	31
4	Germigny-des-Prés plan	32
5	Types of quoining	40
6	Double-splayed window	42
7	Barton-on-Humber plan	44
8	Brixworth church plan	56
9	North Elmham Cathedral plan	60
10	South Elmham, Old Minster plan	62
11	Stow, central crossing plan	64
12	St Michael's church, East Teignmouth	83
13	Banded baluster shaft, Greatham	100
14	Stow, Jews' harp ornament	113

Map 1	England north of the Humber	138
Map 2	England between the Humber and the Thames: the Midland counties	140
Map 3	Lincolnshire	142
Map 4	East Anglia and Essex	144
Map 5	England south of the Thames	146

Preface

This book deals specifically with Anglo-Saxon towers and has only incidental references to the churches to which they may be attached. Such restrictions may perhaps require some justification. Towers are not mere adjuncts to churches; they have specific functions and, one might almost say, personalities of their own. Sometimes the tower is the church, others are free-standing with no adjuncts. Moreover each stage has its own special religious or ecclesiological function. They deserve study as a separate group of buildings independently of the churches to which they may or may not be attached.

An attempt is made to indicate how their structures and functions have developed throughout the centuries, and the sources of the inspiration behind them. This treatment, slender though it is here, is an attempt to avoid that fragmentation of architectural history which is by no means uncommon. This complete unity (more than mere continuity) of architectural history is easy to miss if English architecture is studied alone, as though it had grown up *in vacuo* complete in itself: 'what can one know of England who only England knows?' This failure is plain in the two monumental volumes published in 1964 by H. M. and J. Taylor. These are hardly more than a very detailed descriptive catalogue of Saxon churches. Each church is dealt with as though it had grown up *in vacuo* with little relation to other churches or to anything overseas. The volumes are a valuable source book for facts but lack that coherence which is necessary to a picture of Saxon architectural history.

Two other problems may perhaps be dealt with more conveniently here than in the body of the book: what is a Saxon

9

church, and why are so few still above ground, even in fragmentary condition?

Saxon masons did not all die at Hastings; they continued their work, and their sons and grandsons after them, using their traditional building methods. In some rather backward areas the traditional methods might have continued in use for a century or more after the Conquest, with only minor alterations due to occasional contacts with Norman masons. This was realised by Baldwin Brown who gave the name Saxo-Norman Overlap to the period 1066–c 1100. In this period many Norman and Saxon churches were built and also many churches in which Norman and Saxon details occur together due no doubt to Saxon and Norman masons, or perhaps a Norman master mason with Saxon assistants, being engaged on the same building. As the Overlap period progressed, one would expect such churches to show more and more Norman 'feeling' and less and less Saxon. This is broadly what happened. But this gradual change-over to Norman methods did not take place in a single decade, or half-century; nor did it occur at the same rate everywhere. In more remote parts of the country traditional Saxon building methods persisted long after they had been abandoned elsewhere.

A specific example will illustrate the point—and its importance: the beautiful tower of the church at Bishopstone (plate p 17), near Newhaven, Sussex. It is known that this tower was built in the twelfth century, perhaps in the first half, but maybe nearer the middle than the beginning of the century. Most writers have called it Norman purely on account of its date. But though there is some Norman 'feeling' in the belfry openings, there is not one single specifically Norman feature elsewhere in the tower. If Saxon architecture, like Norman, is a way or manner of building, then Bishopstone tower is a Saxon tower, regardless of its date. If its date were not known it would certainly be considered a typical example of that group of Saxon towers which A. W. Clapham called English Carolingian: its tall, slender proportions, in great contrast to the heavy, low, squat appearance of most Norman parish church towers, its four receding stages separated by string courses, its typically Saxon belfry double openings, proclaim it to be essentially Saxon. Bishopstone might be regarded as chronologically Norman but typologically Saxon; the writer prefers to regard it and similar twelfth century churches as Saxon. It is relevant to point out that no writer has ever suggested that Edward the Confessor's Norman Westminster Abbey was Saxon because it was built before the Conquest. So why should an essentially Saxon tower be called Norman because it was built after AD 1100?

Comparatively few Saxon churches remain today. In H. M. and J. Taylor's monumental descriptive catalogue of Saxon churches (Cambridge, 1964) approximately 400 are listed. This may appear a small number in view of the thousands there must have been in Saxon times. In the Domesday Books of the nine counties of Kent, Surrey, Sussex, Hampshire, Berkshire, Suffolk, Norfolk, Lincolnshire and Northamptonshire the number recorded is nearly 1,400. Not all the then existing churches were recorded and many exist today which are not mentioned in Domesday. Moreover some churches were built after 1086, the date of Domesday Book. Domesday Book was an economic survey, so presumably only those churches would be mentioned which had some economic value such as endowments in land or other property. The total number of churches, many, perhaps a majority, in timber, was clearly very great. Why then have so few of the stone ones survived in view of the excellent building methods of the Saxons.

Some writers appear to think that the great majority of surviving Saxon churches are, 'almost *ex hypothesi*', churches of small, poor communities living in rural, rustic, out-of-the-way areas, and particularly those in the most backward parts of the country, such as Sussex.[1] This implies, erroneously, that the 'great majority' of Saxon churches were of the 'field church' variety, with only a small minority of 'ordinary minsters' and 'lesser churches'.[2] This conclusion does not seem to be consistent with the facts. Sussex was a relatively isolated part of the country, but this applied particularly to the northern and eastern portions where, in consequence, there were and are very few Saxon churches, as there were relatively few Saxon communities. The area was, however, accessible by sea through a number of small ports, and easily accessible from the west. The narrow coastal strip as far east as Brighton and beyond, and the even narrower Arun and Rother valleys which open into it from the north, were and still are crowded with ancient churches. About half the present total of Saxon churches in the county is in this small area.

The two neighbouring wealthy manors of Climping and Lyminster, with two large churches in each, were held directly under the King by Earl Roger, one of the Conqueror's greatest barons. One of these churches still stands; another was monastic. Bosham was one of the wealthiest churches in Saxon England owning 112 hides of land. Bosham, Jevington, Singleton and Sompting have towers; Stoughton has north and south porticus almost large enough to be called transepts and one of the finest chancel arches in the county. Easebourne was later converted to monastic use. Clayton, Hardham, Coombes and others were considered sufficiently important to be beautified internally with very fine eleventh and twelfth century frescoes. There are nearly twenty magnificent chancel arches, three of them among the finest in Saxon England, and highly sophisticated carvings at more than half a dozen. These were not small field churches built for poverty-stricken communities and which except for this would have been rebuilt long since. Many of them, of course, would have been restored and/or partially re-built without losing their essential Saxon character. Otherwise they would have long ago disappeared through natural decay, as have many others. A main cause of the complete disappearance of so many Saxon churches has been their replacement by larger buildings due to increases of population concentrated in what became urban areas: villages which developed into towns, and small towns which became large cities. Thus it is known that there were at least nine churches in the important Saxon borough of Lewes, not one of which is mentioned in Domesday Book, and not one of which exists today. A majority of Saxon churches which have survived have done so because they were built in prosperous villages which have had the subsequent good fortune to escape urbanisation.

An alternative view, not inconsistent with the one developed above and equally valid—indeed both may have been operative —is that of A. H. Allcroft.[3] He writes:

> There can be no doubt that by far the greater number of structural churches existing in England even in the twelfth century were still built of wood only, and this explains the remarkable activity of the church architects of that and the next century: they were replacing in stone the earlier wooden churches and rebuilding on a larger scale some of the few mason built churches already in existence.

In this connection a decree of Archbishop Theodore (669–90) is interesting: that if a church is pulled down or removed the timbers should be used for some other religious purpose. It may well be that when a villein or free man prospered to become eventually a man of property, a minor thegn, he would wish to emphasise his new position by building a church (the Anglo-Saxon equivalent of keeping up with the Jones!). This would normally be of timber and the absolute property of the thegn, who could, if he wished, remove or destroy it. Such churches would probably not be endowed and being of little economic value would not be mentioned in Domesday Book.

E. A. FISHER

October 1968

Part I   Introduction to Anglo-Saxon Towers

Towers, once introduced, became and remained very popular, almost indispensable for all churches except the very small. The tower became the distinguishing ornament of the greater churches and cathedrals. It came to be regarded as something added to the church and no time nor effort was spared to make it elaborate and beautiful, a splendid adornment of God's house. And how well the medieval masons and carvers succeeded. Although they were outside our period, surely few architectural ensembles are more aesthetically satisfying than the three towers of Lincoln Cathedral: their arrangement, their proportions, their ornamentation. They are indeed so well proportioned that it is difficult to realise their size and it may come as a surprise to learn that the great central tower, completed 1307–11 to a height of 268 ft, has an area of cross section not much less than that of a cricket pitch.

We have grown, throughout the centuries, so completely to regard the tower (or towers) as something separate and distinct from the church, desirable but not essential, a dominating element in the church complex, that it is not always realised that towers did not originate in that way, as adjuncts to the church: they were integrated elements in one integrated entity or unity—not a towered church, but a tower-church or (to give it a later, technical name usually reserved for a particular form of this type of church) a turriform church.

CENTRALLY-PLANNED CHURCHES

Centrally planned churches originated in that area which included Syria, Mesopotamia, Armenia, Anatolia—the so-called East Christian area, which formed part of the Eastern Roman or Byzantine Empire. A great variety of church plans developed here, all variants, elaborations or developments of a simple, fundamental type: the centrally planned, four-columned church or 'four poster'. This consisted of a central square, or sometimes circular or polygonal nave, the wall or walls of which were carried up sufficiently high to permit of a range of windows showering light down on the nave, and covered with a dome. There were many variants of this simple plan. The central nave might be surrounded by an aisle or ambulatory, or in lieu of this, apses might project from all four faces of the nave wall; Strzygowski called this a 'niche-buttressed' church as the apses acted as abutments to the nave walls. In other churches the apses might cover the entire width of the wall, producing a quatrefoil enclosing the nave; there were also octofoils as in Constantine's fourth century church at Antioch. Or, and this became the commonest of all forms, there might be intervening straight arms between apses and nave walls, producing a church plan of the form of an equal-armed, Greek cross. In all cases the nave walls had to be higher than the surrounding ambulatory or arms so as to contain the windows to light the central nave. This upper part of the nave wall supported the dome: it might be square, circular or polygonal and was called the drum. It is clear that the simple church was a unity: not a church with a tower but a tower-church, a tower in which the lower portion was the nave, the middle portion a kind of lantern to light the nave and the top portion a protective dome or sometimes a timber roof. The whole entity was in fact a lantern tower and a church. Both ideas have persisted and spread to the West: our modern, beautiful lantern towers, such as Ely, are descended from this early type.

Page 17: (left) Irish round tower, Glendalough, Co Wicklow; *(right)* Bishopstone, Sussex, tower from SW.

Page 18: *(right)* Bywell, St Andrew's tower, upper part from SW; *(below)* Skipwith, tower from SW.

An early example of such a tower is at Alahan Monastir at Kodja Kalessi in Cilicia (southern Asia Minor). This is not a centrally planned church but of modified basilican type. It is one of the earliest towers known, its date being generally accepted as c 450 though some investigators suggest dates up to c 550.[1] The design appears to have been influenced not by Byzantium but by North Syria. Its influence spread westwards, probably via Constantinople, and it reached the West apparently before c 500.[2] How did it get there so quickly? Conant wrote that it was perhaps via Rome due to the flight of artists and craftsmen from Rome at the time of Attila's invasion in the early fifth century; it is known that there was a renewal in architectural and artistic activity in Gaul at about this time. This explanation is not convincing. There appears to be no record of church towers in Rome at this date, nor until much later, except for centrally planned mausolea, of which examples are that of Constantine's daughter, Constantina, c 350, later converted into the baptistery of Sta Costanza, c 432–40, and the problematical S Stefano Rotonda, probably a martyrium, of c 468–83. Milan would appear to be a more likely source. It was an imperial residence after 350 and under its famous bishop Ambrose, 374–397, became the spiritual centre of the western world. It was an architectural centre as well: there were five large churches there in the fourth century (one, S Lorenzo, was a large, centrally-planned quatrefoil, 78 ft across, and 90 ft high, raised above an ambulatory). From Milan the idea may well have passed to Provence, the most Romanised of all the Gaulish provinces, with Arles as its capital in the fifth century. It is known that there were Merovingian churches here: St Pierre at Vienne, fifth to sixth century; the cathedral at Vaison; the abbey at St Victor at Marseilles founded in 414, of which the early crypt remains. These however were probably basilican and there is no evidence of towers. Towers may have reached north-west Europe from Provence via Tours and St Denis near Paris.

A very early monastery, one of the earliest in western Europe and certainly one of the most influential, was at Lérins

on an island near Cannes. It was founded in the early fifth century by St Honoratus who came of a noble family of northern
Gaul. This type of pre-Benedictine monasticism was a new thing
in Europe at this time, a development of the desert anchorite
system of the Egyptian Thebaid. St Patrick (mid fifth century)

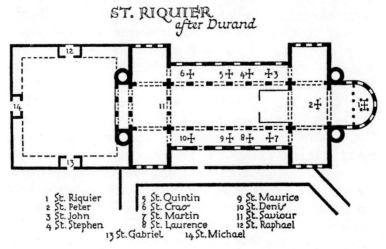

Fig 1. St Riquier (Picardy) plan

probably travelled in Provence and 'the islands of the Tyrrhene
Sea'[3] and may have known Lérins. Certainly he introduced this
type of primitve monasticism into Ireland and regarded its
growth in the Island 'as one of the finest fruits of his missionary work'. But little or nothing is known of the monastic
buildings at Lérins.

   There was a central lantern tower at the second church at St
Denis 754–75, (the predecessor of Suger's famous church of c
1135). Here also, a little later, the west porch may have been
flanked by two square towers. If so, it was one of the earliest
examples of twin western towers in western Europe. This later
became the favourite arrangement of western towers in Germany where, however, single western towers were not unusual.
The two towers at St Denis may have been pylons (see p 27)

Fig 2. St Riquier, lay-out before AD 1090

since they were described by Suger as 'neither very high nor very beautiful.'[4]

They also appeared at St Riquier (Centula) near Abbeville (figs 1 and 2) begun 790 and dedicated in 799, where there were two lantern towers with small open-work stages above, over the two crossings of the eastern and western transepts.

FORTIFIED OR DEFENCE TOWERS

In addition to lantern towers, fortified towers were also built beside churches in Syria in the late Roman period, though they were not common. These too spread to the west and became common in western Europe and Ireland but not apparently in Saxon England. The church was often the largest, sometimes the only, stone building in a district and a natural place of refuge from barbarian and other raiders. The church, however, was vulnerable to fire (often it had a thatched roof), so towers were built (eg, in early Ireland) with doorways eight or ten feet above the ground, accessible only by ladders (see p 77). Such towers could not withstand a siege but were reasonably safe refuges against raiders who came merely to pillage and pass on.

BELL TOWERS

A third type was the bell tower. In the small, early Byzantine churches, bells of cow-bell size were hung above the lantern, or later in a small special roof turret. Bell towers also spread to western Europe. According to Conant[5] all three types of tower were present at the monastic church of St Martin at Tours (built 466–70): a square, fortified western tower, not separate from the church as in Syria, and a low central lantern tower, above which was a small bell turret. It is difficult to accept Conant's early date for the towers of Tours, if there were any. It leaves so little time for these features to travel across Europe from western Asia. He gives no evidence and without that, no independent judgment can be formed. No other examples of such groups of towers of so early a date are known in north-west Europe. The evidence for such early dating is purely literary and Clapham quite fairly pointed out the vagueness and ambiguity of some of the words used: for instance, *turricula* 'might imply anything from a bell cote upwards'. Bells, however, were introduced 'by the end of the sixth, if not in the fifth century.'[6]

By 900, much larger bells were introduced to the West and their inertia was too great for the church building, and especially for the timber towers, so separate belfry towers were built. They were apparently not known in the Eastern Empire where churches and bells were small. C. Ricci[7] asserted that no bell tower was erected in Italy before the second half of the ninth century. The Benedictines, centred at Monte Casino, built the first belfry towers: a square one at S Giovanni, Ravenna, c 893, built on to the early fifth century church,[8] and a similar one at St Pier Maggiore in the same city, of perhaps contemporary date. The earliest free-standing ones are also at Ravenna: at S Apollinare Nuovo (built 526) and S Apollinare in Classe (546–52). These two towers were added four centuries later; they were closely similar, both being detached circular bell towers.[9] Conant thought 'the precedent probably established here created the tradition of free-standing bell towers.'[10] C. Ricci thought they were copied from the two stair turrets of S Vitale in the same city (ded 526: one turret was raised into a tall bell tower in 910).[11] Clapham considered they were copied from the western Carolingian stair turrets which were made before 910.[12] But the Carolingian stair turrets may well have been copied from those at S Vitale, for the plan of Charlemagne's palace chapel at Aachen (792–805) is generally considered to have been based on, though not actually copied from, that of S Vitale. It is known that materials of various kinds, including marble columns, were removed from Ravenna for the building of the chapel. Abbot Odo of Cluny reformed Apollinare in Classe c 936 and the Benedictines took over Apollinare Nuovo in 973 after which date the towers were built.[13] So perhaps both Clapham and Ricci are right.

These towers spread from Ravenna to Lombardy, Rome and throughout Italy where, however, the square form became usual and few were free-standing. The earliest in Italy, outside Ravenna, appears to have been a square one at Sta Maria in Capella, Rome, 1090, which was a precursor of the later Romanesque bell towers of Italy. By the end of the tenth century they had become popular in Burgundy. There was a pair of bell towers at the western facade, flanking the western doors, at the second church at Cluny, 955–80, and at the narthex of St Philibert at Tournus, 990–1019. At Cluny there was also a central lantern tower over the crossing, which appears to have been a lantern-cum-belfry. This arrangement of two western and one central tower became common later but was a novelty in the tenth century. Clapham's view was that western towers need not, perhaps, be looked for in England before the tenth century. This is entirely in accord with the evidence presented by the pre-Conquest remains of this country. Neither of the early groups of churches has any trace of such an appendage, and all the surviving examples bear internal evidence of their late date.[14] Probably few would disagree with that. Literary evidence[15] also supports dates of the second half of the tenth century.

Two lateral towers are recorded at Canterbury, the south one over a porticus containing an altar to St Gregory, generally considered to be one of the period of Bishop Odo, 940–60, but which Gilbert thinks were earlier, in the period 730–867, and most probably of the time of Abbot Wulfred c 813.[16] At Winchester, as rebuilt by Aethelwold (ded 980) there was a tower, staged and open arcaded as at St Riquier. Quoting from a poem by Wolston,[17] Clapham writes of this tower that it was 'in five compartments pierced by open windows on all four sides as many ways are open'. This suggests that the tower was staged. At Glastonbury, Dunstan (c 950) built two porticus against the chancel, and a tower at the east end; the type of tower does not appear to be known. He also built a free-standing tower-chapel (ie, a small turriform chapel) at the west end, apparently the first example in England of two towers in axial relationship (a typical Carolingian feature). At Ramsey Abbey (ded 974) and at Durham (ded 999) there were similar arrangements of two axial towers in the same building (not separate ones, as at Glastonbury). Both apparently were cruciform churches,[18] the eastern tower of each being a central lantern and the western one presumably a bell tower.

STAIRCASE TOWERS

Staircase towers appeared first in the Eastern Empire. Spiral stairs or staircases *(cochleae)* were in use long before separate towers were introduced to house them. A large circular domed structure built c 300 as part of the Emperor Galerius's palace at Salonica, 80 ft across with a wall 18 ft thick at its base, appears to have had a spiral staircase constructed in its wall. (This rotunda was a typical Roman building.) About a century later, in AD 400, it was converted into a church (St George)[19] by the addition of an apsed chancel, an ambulatory and a narthex flanked by staircase towers. Spiral staircases, not towers, were also built in the interior of the outer wall at Sta Costanza, Rome, c 350, and at S Lorenzo, Milan, of c 370, and in a massive pier at St Gerean, Cologne, of c 380.[20] These appear to be the earliest staircase towers recorded. The earliest for our purpose were at S Vitale, Ravenna, 526–47. Here there were two round ones flanking the narthex.[21] There were eight other round towers in Ravenna at about this time. These soon made way in Italy for for the square type but the round persisted elsewhere. It became popular in the Carolingian era. It spread from S Vitale to Charlemagne's palace chapel at Aachen,[22] 792–815. At St Riquier Centula (figs 1 and 2) there were seven: two flanking the apse, two the western vestibule and three at the north, south and west entrances to the western atrium. In these three there were chapels in the upper stages, the earliest examples known of tower chapels.

Round stair towers, also flanking an apse, appeared in the St Gall plan of c 820. Such paired towers[23] were also at Fulda,[24] the early church built by Boniface (Wynfrith) c 751 (the monastery was founded in 744) and rebuilt after 790. They spread further throughout western and north western Europe into France and Germany; for example at St Benigne,[25] Dijon (1001–18), flanking the rotunda; at the eleventh-century Trier cathedral[26] there were at least four minor ones. They reached Spain and Andorra by the second half of the eleventh century, and appeared in late Saxon England at North Elmham in Norfolk, where there was a single one flanking the western tower, of unknown date but probably early eleventh century (see p 60).

PYLONS

The so-called pylons were popular in the East. They were very low, squat (T. G. Jackson called them 'dumpy'), usually square and in pairs flanking a western façade or porch. They occur at the Syrian churches at Tourmanin[27] and Kalb-Lauzeh,[28] both probably sixth century, and at the Armenian cathedral of Ereruk'[29] (fifth to sixth century, or say c 500). A circular pair is at S Vitale (526–47) flanking the eastern apse[30] (the western narthex being flanked by circular stair towers). There was a pair also at S Apollinare-in-Classe, Ravenna[31] (one has been destroyed). These were aisled churches. At Ereruk' and Kalb-Lauzeh the pylons were entered from both aisles and narthex; at Ravenna from narthex only; at S Vitale from the circular ambulatory (aisle).

At Ereruk' there were rather similar, rectangular chambers flanking the apse, both entered from the aisles. At Kalb-Lauzeh there were similar square chambers at the eastern ends of the aisles flanking the narrow, presbyterial space immediately preceding the apse: one was entered from the presbytery, the other from the nave. These eastern chambers, however, were porticus, not pylons.

Pylons appear to have reached North Africa quite early but did not reach western and northern Italy, or did not persist there. They were rare in the West; there may have been a pair at St Denis (see p 20), and very belatedly two pairs were introduced, c 1120 or later, at that French oddity St Front at Perigueux.

The precise use of pylons is not known; possibly they were sacristies of some sort. Certainly they were not the precursors of the Romanesque, paired western towers which appear to have developed independently in the Romanesque period. 'Before the development of heavy peals of bells there was no practical use for pylons on church façades and that is doubtless why the great towers appeared so tardily, after the pylons scheme had passed out of use.'[32]

Part II   Towers in Saxon England

Of the five types of tower already discussed, four eventually reached England. These were: central or lantern towers, western or bell towers, fortified or defence towers, and staircase towers.

1 CENTRAL TOWERS

Centrally-planned churches

Centrally-planned churches of the East Christian type, of which the central tower was the essential structure around which the rest of the church was designed, were rare in England. A very few are recorded in the literatures.

Paulinus built a wooden church or oratory at York in 627 for the baptism of King Edwin of Northumbria. Soon afterwards he built around this wooden structure a stone church described by Bede as square: this was the first cathedral at York. E. C. Gilbert[1] produced considerable literary evidence to suggest that this was an Eastern type of church, definitely more Armenian than Byzantine: probably a square surrounded by aisles, ie, a square within a square, and perhaps with outer porticus, the inner square being raised to tower height to support a dome; the earlier cathedral at Etchmiadzin in Armenia[2] was similar. The York church did not last long. After Edwin's death in battle in 632, Paulinus and his priests (except James, the deacon) fled back to Canterbury with the queen and her family. Little is known of the Church in Northumbria after this until Aidan's mission to Lindisfarne in 634 when a new era of Celtic christianity and wooden churches began and lasted apparently until those great ecclesiastical builders, Benedict Biscop, and Wilfrid of Ripon, re-introduced stone architecture to Northumbria. Wilfrid had been made bishop of all Northumbria by Archbishop Theodore in 669. Before that he had been in Gaul for a year, and as a very young man had spent some years travelling, staying for several periods at Lyons and Rome. By 669 the York church had been for long in a ruinous condition and Wilfrid restored it in 669–71. It was described in glowing terms by Eddius,[3] the enthusiastic admirer and biographer of Wilfrid.

The question may fairly be asked, where did Paulinus get his inspiration to 'build so exceptional a church? He went to Northumbria from Canterbury where there was no central planning. One would have expected him to have built a basilica. Perhaps he did. Bede was familiar only with very long, narrow, high, churches—as at Jarrow where he spent almost the whole of his life, and at Monkwearmouth. A basilica of the Kentish type (with a length-breadth ratio of, say, 1½ to 1) may have seemed to him to be relatively square. Wilfrid's work at York may well have been more than a restoration; possibly a complete rebuilding. He was a great traveller who knew Rome and would have seen the circular baptistery (formerly a mausoleum) of Sta Costanza of c 350, and the supposed martyrium of S Stefano Rotondo[4] (468–83), with their raised tower-like central parts. He was a man who put his ideas into effect on a grand scale. He was a great prelate whose quarrels with his king and Archbishop Theodore showed him to have been aware of his own importance and position. Possibly he was the real builder of this novel, centrally-planned cathedral at York, and later, in 705–9, he built a similar but smaller church at Hexham, St Mary's, to the south-east of his great priory church. It was completed by his successor, Acca, and is mentioned briefly by Eddius and by Richard of Hexham.[5] It had a central space or rotunda, circular or poly-gonal[6] towered in stone or timber, though this is not certainly known. Four arms, or perhaps porticus, projected from the four sides. Richard, who was prior of Hexham from 1142–74, wrote of the church in the past tense so presumably it had disappeared by his time. Like the priory, it had been burnt by the Danes in 875.[7]

These two churches at York and Hexham were certainly the earliest centrally-planned ones in England and perhaps in Western Europe. Gilbert suggests that Charlemagne's palace chapel at Aachen (fig 3), c 790–805, and the church of Germigny-des-Prés (fig 4), of 806,[8] were inspired by York. Alcuin of York was a favourite minister of Charlemagne and a friend

AACHEN

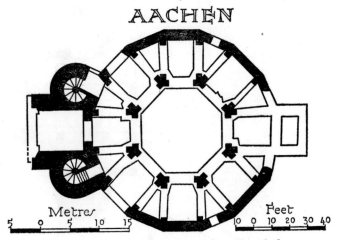

Fig 3. Aachen, Charlemagne's Palace Chapel plan

of Theoduld, the builder of Germigny. This influence may be over-emphasized for Aachen is often stated to have been a poor copy of S Vitale in Ravenna, or at least to have been inspired by it. Charlemagne and his advisers were familiar with the church and looted columns and other materials from Ravenna (probably from Theodoric's palace) for Aachen. But Aachen is certainly not a copy of S Vitale and its many differences were listed by Gilbert.

But the idea of a round church may have come from S Vitale. It has also been stated[9] that Aachen was influenced by the Chrysotriclinion, or audience hall, built by Justin II (565–78) in the precincts of his great palace at Constantinople.

There is evidence for this in the internal arrangements at Aachen, especially in the position of the private apartment, or throne room, above the middle section of the western portion of the ambulatory, where the Emperor could follow the services in seclusion and perhaps have his own private services too. It would seem that the Chrysotriclinion was the ultimate in-

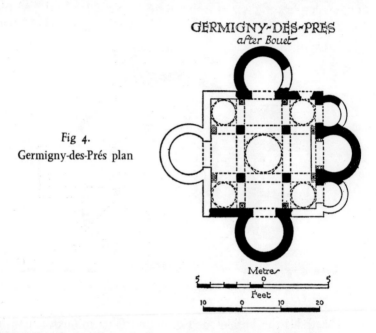

GERMIGNY-DES-PRÉS
after Bouet

Fig 4.
Germigny-des-Prés plan

spiration of the Kaiserhalle in the narthex, which became a common feature in north-western Europe. Gilbert suggests, not unreasonably, that inhabited parts, with chapels, of western towers—usually the second or third stage—are direct offshoots of the Kaiserhalle idea.

It is true that Alcuin may have had an influence too (York cathedral was burnt in 741 but Alcuin probably knew of its general character). All these sets of influences may have been operative at Aachen, for Carolingian architecture was essentially eclectic.

It was rather different at Germigny-des-Prés. Theoduld may

have known Alcuin but he was a Septimanian Visigoth. The horse-shoe arches and horse-shoe planned apses were visigothic features. Moreover one ought not to neglect evidence presented by the contemporary mosaics, which were an integral part of the church. Though sadly defaced and badly restored, they show some influence from Byzantine mosaics via the dome of the Rock at Jerusalem (691), but mostly from Spanish-Jewish illuminated bibles. It is unlikely that the ground plan[10] came from Visigothic Spain where the form was rare, if it occurred at all at this period.[11] The form was common in Armenia from the mid-seventh, until the tenth century,[12] and spread to western Europe where, however, there are few examples: one at Benevento[13] built in 765 by the Lombard king Arachis II, one apparently at Sta Maria delle Cinque Tori at S Germano, near Cassino (now destroyed),[14] (778–93), and one at S Satiro, Milan of 868.

There were two small ones closely resembling Germigny, and almost contemporary with it (c 800) at Malles (S Benedetto) with horse-shoe arches and at nearby Münster in Grunbünden—Grisons—without horse-shoe arches.[15] The arches at Malles suggest that the influence here was from, not to, Germigny. It seems likely that the Germigny ground plan was carried westward from Armenia by emigrant craftsmen and masons, for the Armenians were great traders and travellers. It may seem doubtful that either Aachen or Germigny was influenced by the church at York. These three churches were similar in their superstructures: four-armed, centrally planned, with raised central towers, perhaps supporting domes. The literary evidence for domes is interesting but by no means convincing. It seems more likely that they were timber roofed. The ground plans differed widely: York, according to Gilbert, was a square within a square with outer porticus; Aachen was an octagon within a sedecagon; Germigny was a Greek cross, with a central tower, perhaps domed, and with the four corner angle spaces between the arms filled with low square chambers. The ground plan was square, the plan of the second stage was a cross, a member of that group of church types known as cross-in-square, cross inscribed, by French writers as *croic inscrite*, and by Conant quincunx.

A quincunx is an arrangement of five things so placed as to occupy each corner and the centre of a square. A quincunx church is described by Krautheimer as, 'a structure divided into nine bays, the centre being a large square, the corner bays small squares, the remaining four bays rectangular; the centre bay, resting on four columns, is domed, the corner bays are either domed or groin vaulted, the rectangular bays are as a rule barrel vaulted.'[16] The history of the quincunx form is obscure. It was used in some non-ecclesiastical buildings in the near East as early as the late second century. It appeared in ecclesiastical buildings in the near East, and in western Europe in the late eighth or early ninth century, although it was apparently known in Armenia by the mid-seventh century. In the West, one of the earliest was at Germigny (c 806) and there was a similar one at S Satiro, Milan in 868.

This specific Eastern—certainly more Armenian than Byzantine—influence in north-west Europe, whether it came direct or, as E. C. Gilbert suggests from pre-Carolingian England, may perhaps best be regarded as an interesting but minor factor in the development of Carolingian architecture. Undoubtedly the really important and architecturally influential early Carolingian churches were basilican and usually cruciform; eg, the Abbey churches of St Denis (cons 775), St Riquier (begun c 790) and Fulda (cons 819).

A religious foundation existed in Bath for a century or more before 781 when the monastery, possibly a cell of Worcester, was acquired from bishop Heathered by King Offa of Mercia, who, sometime about 790, built the church.[17] It must have been a large church for King Edgar was crowned in it before a great congregation in 973.[18] Also it was stated in a charter of King Eadwig dated 957:[19] '*Quod in Bathonia mira fabrica constructem cognoscitur*,' which suggests that to the King or his scribe, it appeared to be the most extraordinary piece of

Page 35 : *(left)* Jarrow, tower belfries from SE; *(right)* Barton-on-Humber, tower from SW.

Page 36: Above: *(left)* Skipwith, tower arch from nave; *(right)* Canterbury, St Mildred's nave, megalithic quoins. Below: Barton-on-Humber: *(left)* lower part of tower S face; *(right)* tower N doorway.

architecture he had ever seen. This view is strengthened by the tenth century seal, still extant, which shows three tall apses with elongated pilaster strips on their exteriors. The foundations of a semi-circular apse, presumably Saxon, were excavated in 1833 immediately to the east of the east window of the existing Perpendicular church, which replaced the late eleventh century Norman church.[20] The two other apses may be under the bases of the former Norman tower supports.

This curious east end is similar to that of St Donatus at Zadar in Dalmatia,[21] which, however, had tall recesses instead of pilasters. This church was explored and described in detail by Sir Thomas Jackson.[22] It was a circular, two storied building with no exterior ambulatory—the church proper, with a gallery in lieu of the usual ambulatory, being on the second floor. It is of the type of S Vitale, of Charlemagne's palace chapel at Aachen, and of Germigny-des-Prés, but differs from all three in many important respects. In view of the similarity of the two east ends, it is tempting to accept Bath, the earlier of the two, as a centrally planned church like Zadar, in which case it would be unique in Saxon England. But from a close study of a measured plan of the church, it is difficult to fit Zadar into the compass of the present lay-out. Bath could, however, have been similar to Wilfrid's churches at Hexham and York, or to Germigny-des-Prés or to Alfred's church at Athelney (though this was a century later). Such a plan would almost certainly have been familiar to Offa. No other monumental remains have been exposed to support this view, or any other; the church may even have been an aisled basilica, though this would have been unusual at this date. So because of the lack of evidence, no opinion is justified as to the type it was, though a centrally planned church like Germigny seems an attractive conjecture. The church was certainly unusual; the three tall apses on the seal, with their suggestion of Eastern influence, bring it into line with the interesting buildings which preceded it in Northumbria.[23] The problem of the identity of the actual builder remains.[24]

c

There is no record of any similar, centrally planned church in England until Alfred built his church at Athelney, which was almost certainly a copy of, or inspired by, the church at Germigny-des-Prés.

An abbey church was built at Abingdon, c 960, by Abbot Ethelwold. It is stated[25] to have had a round chancel, a round nave and a round tower, and this suggests that it was probably centrally planned, perhaps with a central round nave with apses of considerable projection to east and west. A curved piece of masonry was dug up in 1922, which may have been a portion of an apse. The predecessor of this church, built by the thegn Heane (c 675–80), was a long church of 120 ft with apses at east and west. This is the first mention of double apses in western Europe—a century before the feature appeared in Carolingian architecture. Double apses were known in Syria from the fifth or sixth century so the idea may have reached England via Archbishop Theodore's (668–90) ecclesiastical invasion. It is possible that this earlier church may have influenced the design of Ethelwold's church.

A similarly planned tomb-chapel was built at Bury St Edmunds in the tenth century as the grave of St Edmund, the East Anglian king who was killed by the Danes in 869. Within forty years he had become the centre of a cult and was honoured as a saint in East Anglia. Remains were discovered in 1275 when the Lady Chapel was built, but apart from this site—and some remains of the chapel—nothing else is known of it.

The bishop's palace at Hereford was another centrally planned church. It was built by Bishop Robert of Loraine, 1079–95, and was ultimately derivative from Charlemagne's palace chapel at Aachen, the precursor of the *doppel-capellen*—double (palace) chapels, of Western Germany. These chapels, at first circular or polygonal, were replaced in the late eleventh century by square, two-storied buildings. The Hereford chapel was, like Germigny-des-Prés, a square within a square, ie, a quincunx church; the four corner piers of the inner square supported an upper storey which acted as a gallery overlooking the square central well; above this was a lantern. The upper stage was for the use of the family, the ground floor for the retainers. This chapel was largely pulled down in the eighteenth century.

The only other centralised building was the great rotunda begun but not completed, by Abbot Wulfric (1047–59) of St Augustine's, Canterbury. His intention was to unite the two Augustan churches of SS Peter and Paul and St Mary by pulling down the east end of one and the west end of the other (and eventually to rebuild both) by means of a great rotunda. It had not risen far above ground at Wulfric's death in 1059 and the later abbot Scotlaud (1070–87) in his general re-building destroyed all that was above ground. What is left is the crypt, octagonal without, circular within, with a central ring of eight massive rubble piers separating the central circle from a narrow ambulatory. It was over 65 ft across with walls 5 to 8 ft thick. There were two massive semi-circular towers attached to the north and south sides (as at St Benigne, Dijon, built 1001–18) but it is not known whether these were intended to be staircase towers. There seems little doubt however that Wulfric's design, though simple, was based on that of St Benigne.[26]

Quoining

Quoining is the strengthening of corners of buildings by specific treatment with relatively large stones. Such strengthening is especially necessary with rubble or flint walls since owing to the irregular shapes and sizes of rubble, no bonding-in is practicable. In some areas where suitable stone is not available, the corners are constructed of selected flattish rubble stones, or even ordinary rubble indistinguishable from the walling. In some areas, eg, East Anglia, the quoining problem is solved by building circular towers. Normally however various types of stones in various arrangements were used (fig 5). The main types were:

Megalithic quoins (plate p 36) are of large stones of up to 4 ft by 1–2½ ft. They may or may not be dressed on the two exterior faces, and may be piled on one another in no orderly arrangement: a good example is at St Mildred's, Canterbury.

Slab quoins, or big stone work, are more sophisticated than the megalithic type. The stones are rectangular though occasionally square-sectioned and up to 2 ft or more long by 10 in or so wide and laid flat on their sides (side alternate) or faces (face alternate) with their long faces on alternate faces of the wall: thus on a tower south-west quoin, one long face would lie N–S, the one above E–W and so on. Good examples are at Stow (Lincs) and Norton (co Durham).

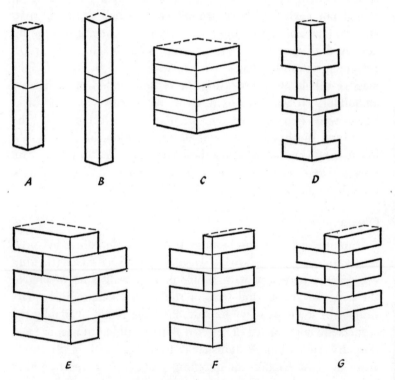

Fig 5. Types of quoining:

(*a*) pillar quoins
(*b*) true long and short work
(*c*) clasping quoins
(*d*) regular upright and flat

(*e*) face alternate
(*f*) side alternate
(*g*) dovetail quoins

A variant of this type is close to the megalithic and might be regarded as intermediate. In these, massive stones up to 3 ft high are employed on end, and between each pair of stones is a thin clasping or binding-in stone. Good examples are at Brigstock (plate p 54) and Earls Barton (Northants). This type is common in the jambs of tower arches where they may consist of massive through-stones almost as high as the opening, with flat slabs lying above, as at Earls Barton and Monkwearmouth's western openings.

The so-called *Long and Short Quoins* are of two main types and one sub-type:

(a) Regular Upright and Flat,
(b) Hidden Upright and Flat, or Apparent or Pseudo Long and Short,
(c) True Long and Short.

Regular Upright and Flat Quoins consist of rectangular or square-sectioned stone strips up to 4 ft long by 6 or 8 in wide; there is much variation in the individual sizes. The stones are bedded in on edge and may or may not project from the wall surface to the intended depth of plaster. Between each pair of uprights is a comparatively large, (superficially) square or squarish thin slab, about 6 or 8 in high by 2 ft or so square, laid flat and built into the wall—as it were to tie in the angle. Good examples are at Rockland All Saints (Norfolk) and Market Overton (Rutland). This is the type first noticed by Thomas Rickman[27] in 1835 and called by him 'Long and Short', a name used in the earlier literature and sometimes today. But this term is better reserved for another type of genuine 'long and short' described below, not apparently known to Rickman. The ambiguity was pointed out by Baldwin Brown who introduced the term 'upright and flat' for the type just described.

A sub-group of this type may be called *Hidden Upright and Flat* or Apparent or Pseudo Long and Short. This is structurally identical with Regular Upright and Flat but the exterior edges of the flats (and sometimes of the uprights, to make them appear of uniform width throughout) are cut back to the level of the wall surface so that when the wall was plastered the quoins would look like genuine Long and Short though they are in fact Upright and Flat. To-day, with much of the old plaster

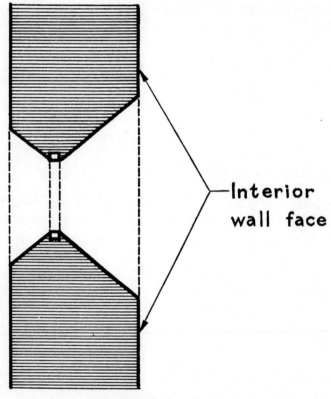

Fig 6. Double-splayed window

stripped from the walls, they would be indistinguishable from Regular Upright and Flat if it were not for the recessed, cut-back edges. Good examples are at Barnack, Northants (plate p 89) and St Benet's, Cambridge (plate p 90).

True Long and Short Quoins consist of rectanglar or square-sectioned stone strips 2 to 4 ft long and about 6 or 8 in laterally bedded on end and often projecting from the wall surface. Between each pair of longs or uprights is a short length of stone strip of similar cross section to the longs. This type is now more usual with pilaster work than with quoins owing to the greater strength of the other types which makes them more suitable for quoining. A good example of this type is at Worth (Sussex).

Turriform churches

Another and quite different type of centrally planned church which persisted well into the Norman period occurs in Saxon England. The Eastern type was designed on a circular axis. On entering the church one could turn left or right and walk round the church to the east end. The long-naved cruciform church, so familiar in western Europe, was designed on a longitudinal axis: on entering the church one could walk straight ahead through the nave to the chancel. There is a centrally planned type of church designed not on a circular but on a longitudinal axis. In such, the nave is the ground floor of the tower, the upper two stages of which are the lantern and belfry respectively. There was a short chancel projecting from the east face and a similar projection—a west-work—from the west face of the tower. The function of the west-work is not known: it may have been used as a porch, or sacristy, or porticus, or in some areas for the use of catechumens not yet admitted to the full rites of the church. Such churches are known as turriform.

The best example of this type in England is at Barton-on-Humber (Lincs) (fig 7, plates pp 35 and 36) supposedly of the tenth century[28] though a date of the time of Canute (1017–35) seems more likely.[29] Baldwin Brown dates it to mid-eleventh century. The tower is decorated with pilaster strip work (like Earls Barton and Barnack, and some others) and has openings on all four sides. The north and south doorways are small: round-headed on the south and gable-headed on the north. They are near the west end, opposite each other; ie, in positions common in Saxon naves. On the west is a large round-headed door-

way leading from the west-work which also had a large doorway
(now blocked) in its west wall; ie, it had its own doorway from
the exterior. In the east wall is a large round-headed arch leading into the nave, ie, now a tower arch, but originally a chancel
arch. The original chancel was replaced later by the existing
nave (much wider than the tower) and chancel. There are vertical roughnesses on the tower east wall (east face) which indicate
where the north and south walls of the early narrow chancel

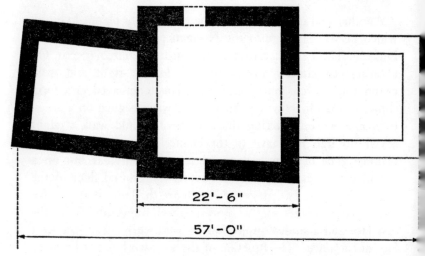

Fig 7. Barton-on-Humber, turriform church plan

were torn away when the later nave was built, and that the
chancel was narrower than the tower. On this east wall too,
seen from the nave, the north-east and south-east tower quoins
are visible, extending to the ground. Both features indicate the
turriform character of the original church. Another indication
of this is the square-cut pilaster strip-work round the heads and
down the jambs of both the eastern arch and western doorway,
but on the west face only of the eastern arch and on the east
face only of the western doorway, ie, on the tower face of each
opening where it would be visible to the congregations assembled
in the tower-nave.

Broughton-by-Brigg (Lincs) was also turriform, but apparently had no west-work. Later, but still in the Saxon period, a circular stair tower was attached to the west face of the tower. The south doorway is unusually close to the south-west corner, again normal for a nave doorway, and there is no north doorway. As at Barton, the more elaborate face of the tower arch (formerly the chancel arch) faces the west where the congregation would be. The original chancel was replaced later by a Norman nave and chancel.

Earls Barton (Northants) (plates p 90), was almost certainly turriform, but without any western annexe; the rich pilaster ornament covering the whole western and other faces precludes the possibility of an annexe. The doorway is in the west wall, and there is no north or south doorway. The chancel was replaced, c 1100, by a Norman nave and chancel. The tower arch leading to the nave was much altered in Norman times and again in the thirteenth century, and provides no information concerning its predecessor. The eastern quoins, of upright and flat work, visible from the nave, are complete to the ground; this indicates that the church was turriform and the original chancel was narrower than the tower.

Another turriform church was at Eastdean (East Sussex). Most writers consider this an early Norman church. It was built probably c 1100 and the quoining is of Norman type, fairly small, almost cubical stones, but with no tooling. But the small blocked south doorway is of specifically Saxon type: the west jamb is of two tall stones, about 2 ft 6 in high; the east jamb of one tall stone c 4 ft high with one short one of 11 in above it. The Normans did not use such massive stones in any of their stone work so, in the writer's opinion, the church is Saxon, despite its date. Sussex was the most backward, architecturally and culturally, of the Saxon kingdoms and was the last to accept Christianity. Because it had no large quarries of good building stone, it did not develop schools of mason craft such as arose at famous quarries in other areas, such as Purbeck (Dorset) and Barnark (Northants). Saxon masons in Sussex continued to use the methods of their forefathers long after these methods had been abandoned elsewhere. Probably in no other county are there so many post-Conquest, even post-1100, churches built in the Saxon manner and which—if Saxon architecture, like Norman is a manner of building—should properly be regarded as Saxon.

Originally the church at Eastdean consisted of a square tower, 11 ft 11 in N–S by 11 ft 8½ in E–W on the interior, with walls only 3 ft to 3 ft 2 in thick—definitely not a Norman thickness —and an eastern semi-circular apsidal chancel. There was no west-work nor western opening (the existing doorway is modern), the only entrance being in the south wall, a little west of central. Like many Saxon towers, it is of three slightly recessed stages, separated by string courses. The apse no longer exists but its plan is evident on the ground to the east of the tower and there are marks of it on the exterior of the tower east wall. The arch, now built up, leading to the apse, is of one order of rather small voussoirs, not through-stones, with some diagonal tooling, showing Norman 'feeling'. Turriform churches persisted after the Conquest. There is one of definitely Norman date at Fingest (Bucks).

Cruciform churches

We have little information about the great minsters and cathedrals as so many were destroyed, to be replaced by the great Norman cathedral and abbey churches. In the tenth century abbey church at Peterborough (Medeshamstede), remains of which are to be seen below the nave of Peterborough Cathedral, the excavated foundations show no indication of a central tower, though it may have had a western one: a tower was *gehalgod*, consecrated, in 1059 (A-S Chronicle). Western and central towers in the same church were rare: there are literary references to such in a very few churches, eg, Ramsey Abbey (Hunts), dedicated in 974, and at the Saxon cathedral at Durham consecrated in 999.

Some writers[30] think towers were intended over the central presbyterial spaces at Deerhurst (Glos) and Brixworth (Northants) (fig 8). It is not known whether one was intended at Stanton Lacy (Salop), which has a north but not a south transept, the present tower being later. One was clearly intended at Stow (Lincs) over its truly magnificent central crossing.

A central tower almost implies a four-armed church, whether centrally planned, as in the East, or the western basilican long-naved, cruciform or transeptal church. Those given above are cruciform: ie, they have either north and south transepts or porticus. In England, two-celled churches consisting of nave and chancel, without porticus or transepts, sometimes had towers in a central position but not wider than the nave, as at Dunham Magna (Norfolk). These, however, are not really central towers (which always had lateral supports in the form of porticus or transepts), but axial towers (see p 59).

There are some interesting differences worthy of notice between Saxon central towers. At Norton (co Durham), Stow (Lincs), Restenneth Abbey (Forfar), Wootton Wawen (Warwicks), Great Tey (Essex) and formerly at Sherborne Abbey (Dorset), the central towers were wider than the four arms of the church; in those at Dover, Breamore (Hants) and Repton (Derbys) the towers are wider than the chancel but the same width as the nave. The Norton tower is about 15 ft 6 in square and about 40 ft high, with walls 3 ft thick, the transept wall being 2 ft 6 in. Such thickening of tower walls to support the greater mass was common but not universal. At Repton the tower was 24 ft N–S by 25 ft E–W; there was no thickening. At Stow (fig 11) the crossing walls were 4 ft 5 in thick, the transept walls only 2 ft 6 in. Such a crossing was clearly intended to support a tower. It was square, 14 ft 3 in between the jambs, and the arches were about 30 ft high. At Breamore (plate p 136) the tower western quoins extend to the ground; at Dover the quoins do not extend below nave roof level, below which the tower and nave walls are continuous like those of an axial tower.

At Wootton Wawen the four arms are of later date (not Saxon) than the slender tower, which is only about 14 ft 6 in square on the interior. The tower has the quite unusual wall thickness of 2 ft 3 in; the existing, later, nave walls are 2 ft 10 in thick; the original Saxon walls would not have been more than 2 ft 3 in. Apparently there was no thickening of tower walls here.

At Great Tey the tower was about 18 ft square with walls 4 ft thick. At Restenneth Abbey the tower was about 10 ft 4 in square and 50 ft high, and the walls 2 ft 8 in thick.

At Hadstock (Essex), originally with either porticus or transepts, there is no central tower (only a later western one) though one was probably intended; the nave wall, about 2 ft 6 in thick, is (and was originally) thickened at the transept opening to about 3 ft evidently to support a tower.

2 BELL TOWERS

Once introduced, bell towers became popular in Saxon England, mainly as single western towers. Twin western towers, common in Germany, the Rhineland and France, are not known to occur at all in Saxon England. Excluding round towers which, though bell towers, are in a class apart and require separate treatment, there are about 112–15, including a few doubtful ones, existing in whole or in part. A few are not at the west end. At Kingsdown (Kent) the tower is on the south, overlapping nave and chancel, a position commonly occupied by porticus. Possibly originally there was a porticus here, raised later into a tower, as at Stoughton (Sussex) where there is a fourteenth century tower over an eleventh century south transept. At Little Snoring (Norfolk) is a south-west detached round tower. There are later, post-Saxon, towers at West Stoke (Sussex) off the west end of the south wall, and a Norman one off the east end of the south wall at Westhampnett (Sussex).

Western towers may conveniently be studied in two groups: porch towers and '*de novo*' towers.

Porch towers

At seven churches, all dating back to the Early Saxon Period (ie, to the pre-Danish invasions of 866–886) there were western porches on which later, in the Late Saxon Period, towers were erected. These are Corbridge (Northumberland), Jarrow and Monkwearmouth (Co Durham), Bardsey and Ledsham (Yorkshire, West Riding), Brixworth (Northants) and Deerhurst (Glos). These form a small group which require separate comment. The porches were originally of one or two stages and as they were not intended to support towers (at that period un-

49

known in England) had walls no thicker, and sometimes thinner, than the nave, and rarely more than 2 ft 7 in. They are rectangular in plan and usually have their longer axes lying east-west. Their external width is generally less than the interior width of the nave; ie, they have the same lateral dimensions as the porches supporting them.

At Corbridge the tower is about square on the exterior, but all the sides are of different lengths indicating the bad setting-out common in Saxon churches; the N–S dimensions are: west wall 10 ft 11½ in, east wall 10 ft 7 in; E–W dimensions are: north wall 11 ft 1½ in, south wall 11 ft 5 in. The walls are about 2 ft 7 in thick, approximately 4 in less than the nave west wall to north and south of the tower.

At Jarrow (plate p 35) the tower was erected c 1075 by Abbot Aldwine who rebuilt the monastery and ruined church which had been burnt by the Danes in 794 and 866 and again by William the Conqueror in 1069–70. It is rectangular; the lowest stage is 21 ft 3 in N–S by 13 ft E–W, the longer axis being N–S, a great contrast to the usual porch towers. E. C. Gilbert[1] makes out a strong case for the theory that the original porch was (a part of) a narthex extending the whole width of the original nave—now the chancel—and that Aldwine built his tower on and to the plan of the narthex. The tower originally had three stages, the top one being Aldwine's belfry. A little later a fourth stage, another belfry, was added, separated from the third by a string course, just below which the rectangular tower is made more square by three-stepped off-sets on the north and south walls; this seems to suggest that, to the builders, the tower appeared to be of unusual shape.

At Monkwearmouth (plate p 108) the original (seventh century) porch was apparently a little later than the nave for it is built against the west wall with a straight joint, ie, not bonded in. It was of one stage. The walls were only 1 ft 9 in thick, thinner than the nave wall (2 ft ½ in). Its internal dimensions were 8 ft 2½ in N–S by 9 ft 5 in E–W, with the longer axis E–W, and is much narrow than the interior nave width which was rather less than 20 ft. Four stages were added later, first a second stage to the porch, perhaps between 710 and 735, and then three more stages probably by Aldhune, bishop of Chester-le-Street, c 990–5, making a tower of five stages rising to a height of 60 ft.[2] The stages are separated by string courses but there are no off-sets, ie, recessing of stages. The top stage is the belfry. None of the stages was bonded in. It was discovered during the repairs of 1924–5 that the tower had become inclined westwards, out of vertical, leaving a gap of some inches at the top between it and the nave wall. In view of the thin walls and the lack of bonding, the fact that the tower has remained in being for nearly a thousand years is a great compliment to Saxon workmanship, to Saxon foundations and Saxon mortar.

At Bardsey the original porch, probably contemporary with the nave, of pre-870 date, is 10 ft 2½ in E–W and 8 ft N–S internally, with walls 2 ft ½ in thick—the same as the nave wall. It has no exterior string course dividing it into stages, but stages are indicated by the three ranges of openings above the porch (internal timber floors were inserted later). The second and third stages have walls of about the same thickness as the porch; the fourth, ie, the belfry stage, has walls only 1 ft 8 in thick.

At Ledsham the upper half is a Norman tower raised on a two-staged Saxon porch. The internal dimensions are 12 ft 3 in E–W by 9 ft 8 in N–S which suggest a porch tower. Baldwin Brown denied this but H. M. Taylor[3] demonstrated conclusively that the lower half was a porch: the walls are thin, only 2 ft and are not bonded into the nave wall which suggests that the porch was later than the nave, but not much later for the two are similar in fabric and type of openings.

The tower of Deerhurst is of quite unusual interest.[4] It was originally a two-staged porch, dated by Gilbert to the first half of the eighth century. Like Jarrow, it is markedly rectangular but in an east-west, not north-south direction. Its dimensions are 21 ft 6 in E–W by 14 ft 6 in N–S. This rectangularity seems to be original, for a little later in the Saxon period both stages were divided internally N–S by a mid-wall into two unequal sections, an eastern one approximately 8 ft 9 in square and a western one 8 ft 9 in by 5 ft 3 in. Later, but also in the Saxon period, a third stage was added, dated by Gilbert to some time between mid-eighth and mid-ninth centuries. This stage contains the well known, massive gable-headed double opening, its sill 28 ft above floor level. Gilbert thinks this was used, even definitely built, as a chapel. Later still, in the Late Saxon Period, probably in the tenth century, two more stages were added making five in all forming a tower about 70 ft high. The top stage was the belfry. The walls are about 2 ft 8 in thick, only slightly thicker than the nave walls which vary between 2 ft 3 in and 2 ft 6 in. The top parapet between two string courses, and capping are post-Saxon; there are no string courses in the five Saxon stages.

At Brixworth (fig 8; plate p 89) the early porch was of two stages, contemporary with the nave, and unlike most Saxon porches, was longer N–S than E–W; ie, its longer axis does not lie east-west. It is, however, much narrower than the nave. Its external dimensions are 21 ft 6 in N–S by 20 ft E–W; internally they are 15 ft and 12 ft 5 in which make the walls average 3 ft 3 in thick N–S and 3 ft 8½ in in E–W, and not very dissmilar from the nave walls which are about 3 ft 8 in. Later the porch was converted into a tower by the addition of at least two stages, resulting in a tall tower which 'could hardly have been less than 70 ft' (Gilbert). The circular staircase tower, attached to the west face of the tower, was built at the same time. Baldwin Brown and Clapham dated these additions to the mid-tenth century, A. Hamilton Thompson[5] to the mid-eleventh 'or even rather later'. E. C. Gilbert,[6] in a recent (1965) study of the church, gives evidence which suggests a later date than that hitherto accepted for the main fabric of the church and an earlier one for the tower. He thinks it improbable that the existing church is the same as the church built by a few monks from Peterborough c 670. This agrees with the views of A. H. Allcroft.[7] Gilbert suggests a more likely date for the church between 750 and 810 with some certainty, he prefers 750–770.

Page 53: *(below)* Haddiscoe, tower from NW; *(right)* Roughton, tower from N.

Page 54: Above: (left) Bolam, S belfry opening with corbelled-out capital; (right) Brigstock, tower S window and nave SW quoin from S aisle. Below: (left) Monkwearmouth, many banded baluster in W porch; (right) Deerhurst, openings above tower arch from E.

He dates the tower to c 800–820. His evidence is strong but he seems to be on less firm ground when he adds that 'there is no sign that Brixworth ever had a belfry tower' and that the Brixworth tower is 'the first known example of the tall western tower, not yet a belfry, in England.'

There seems to be no history of western towers not being belfries; no hint is given by such scholars as Conant and Krautheimer of the existence anywhere in Europe of non-belfry western towers. However, they do not specifically deny the existence of non-belfry western towers. The square dumpy ones at Corbie of c 885 may have been pylons. Moreover, what would be the purpose of such towers? It is true that 810 is too early a date to be acceptable to present general opinion for a bell tower as it is nearly a century before large bells were introduced to the West and more than a century before the first appearance of bell towers in Burgundy at the second church of Cluny,[8] 955–81, or before Clapham's date for their introduction into England, 'not perhaps before the tenth century'.

There is certainly a problem here. As so often in this kind of historical work the apparent solution of one problem raises another—or others. This new problem must remain for the time being. But Dr Gilbert may well be right. The only evidence against the idea is the lack of positive evidence for it. In the solution of any problem there has to be a first step. Dr Gilbert's idea may be that first step.

A fourteenth century rectangular tower was raised over the rectangular western adjunct at Westdean (East Sussex). There is a late Norman one above the Saxon west porch at Sullington (West Sussex) and it seems more likely that this was a Norman replacement of a Saxon belfry, for the lowest stage is as wide as the nave, as no porch would be.

At Titchfield (Hants) the porch, perhaps of two stages, was dated by the *Victoria County History* to the late ninth century or earlier, and by Baldwin Brown to the late eighth or early ninth. A. R. Green[9] suggests that it may well be of the late seventh century, part of one of Wilfrid's churches. It is certainly

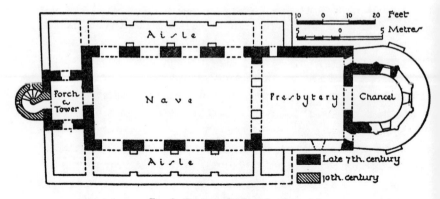

Fig 8. Brixworth church plan

very early; its quoins are megalithic and its walls only 2 ft 3 in thick. The tower was added probably in the twelfth century and the spire in the fifteenth.

It is likely that there were two porch-towers at the Saxon cathedral at Canterbury, destroyed in the 1067 fire. These appear to have been raised over the two—north and south—porticus, during the restoration of the cathedral by Archbishop Odo, 940–60.

All other towers were built *de novo* from the ground. As the lateral dimensions were not determined by those of any under-lying porch, they were normally larger than porch towers. They were narrower than the nave, ie, the external north-south width was less than that of the nave though often greater than the nave internal width; the nave wall projects north and south of the tower and has its own quoins to the ground. Further, where-as porch towers were usually rectangular, as the porches were, with their longer axis east-west, *de novo* towers approximated to square, a few only being markedly rectangular.

English Carolingian towers

Excluding porch towers, turriform churches and axial towers, there are about ninety western towers. These are sometimes divided into two groups, those called by Clapham, English Carolingian towers and those Baldwin Brown called Lincoln-shire Bell towers.

The former type was derived from the crossing towers of St Riquier dated 790–800. This church had nine towers two of which were round or octagonal over the crossings of the eastern and western transepts. The eastern one was a central tower with transepts acting as abutments. The one nearer the west end was similar, with transept abutments; ie, in spite of its position it was really a central tower, like its axial twin, between two transepts. Above the drums—the lanterns with round windows —were three receding, arcaded openwork stages. These stages were relatively tall and slender, giving a spire-like appearance to the structure, and were certainly of timber. Each open stage was recessed considerably behind the one below (figs 1 and 2).[10]

That such towers reached England is certain from literary references. One of two markedly receding stages is shown on the thirteenth century seal of Chichester Cathedral:[11] a central tower with single-staged belfry above. Another is on the early twelfth century seal attached to an Exeter church of 1133. The timber upper stage (the belfry) at Breamore (Hants) (plate p 136), though later, may well be a reproduction of an original timber recessed belfry, based on the St Riquier model, as also may be the short timber belfry at Wotton (Surrey). From literary sources too there was a great five-staged open-work tower at Ethelwold's cathedral at Winchester dedicated in 980, but completed later, which from the rather vague writing[12] appears to have been similar to those at St Riquier. This recessing of stages, though generally only slight, remained a characteristic of Saxon western towers. About half of those still existing are of this type: two to four stages, slightly recessed and separated by string courses.

Among these English Carolingian towers is a small sub-group with exteriors richly decorated with pilaster strip work (see pp 116–20). These include: Barnack and Earls Barton (Northants) (plates pp 89, 90), Barton-on-Humber (Lincs) (plates pp 35, 36),

Sompting (Sussex) (plate p 134), and to a lesser degree, on the top stages only: Stowe-nine-Churches (Northants), St Benet's (Cambridge) (plate p 90) and Langford (Oxon).

Lincolnshire bell towers

This group of western towers were so called as they are characteristic of that county. It is not known whether they originated there but nearly all towers in Lincolnshire are of this type and, though not confined to the county, they are relatively less numerous in other parts of the country. The walls, of rubble, rise vertically upwards with no batter, though in a few a very slight narrowing upwards is found: eg, at Marton (Lincs). At St Michael's (Oxford) (plate p 136) there is no exterior batter but the walls thin upwards internally by about 1 ft which serves the same purpose. In height and wall thickness they are comparable with other western towers; in thickness very few of either kind approach Norman, eg, St Michael's Oxford 4 ft at base thinning to about 3 ft, Earls Barton 4 ft thinning to about 2 ft 6 in, Clapham (Beds) 4 ft thinning slightly upward. Caistor (Lincs) is exceptional; the south wall is 3 ft 8 in thick, the north wall 4 ft 11 in, the east wall is 5 ft 9 in—5 ft 11 in and the west wall 3 ft 10 in; the east wall is about 2 ft thicker than any other in the county. The quoins are usually of fairly large oblong blocks laid with their broad faces arranged in alternate wall faces, ie, in side-alternate arrangement, suggesting the common Anglo-Saxon 'upright and flat' work though the heights of the blocks are comparable. These blocks, though smaller than Saxon megalithic or big-stone work, are larger than typical Norman quoin stones which usually approximate to small stone cubes. In a few, including Caistor, large, irregular, roughly square, blocks are used.

These towers are almost square in plan and of tall slender proportions; the most typical in general appearance are perhaps St Mary-le-Wigford and St Peter-at-Gowts (plate p 72), Lincoln and Rothwell (Lincs). Some measure no more than ten or eleven feet along each interior axis. In the few rectangular ones the longer axis may lie east-west though in a very few it may be north-south, as at Caistor and Nettleton (Lincs). Most are of two stages, a very tall lower one, with short belfry above, separated by a string course. There are exceptions: there are partial remains of a second string at Clee (north wall), Rothwell (south wall) and Nettleton (north and south); there are three stages separated by two strings at Hough-on-the-Hill, Thurlby and Syston; Caistor has four stages and three strings; at Great Hale and Springthorpe there is no string and no recessing of the belfry (all these are in Lincs). In Lincolnshire the double heads of the belfry openings do not go straight through the walls but are backed by flat stone slabs, ie, internal thin lintels. Below these openings the windows are of the narrow loop kind, single-splayed internally, and externally of key-hole shape.

In short, it may be said that these Lincolnshire bell towers show no specifically Saxon features, except the actual belfry double openings, but also no specifically Norman features. At Clapham (Beds) (plate p 133), and Wharram-le-Street (Yorkshire, East Riding), both of post-Conquest date, the belfry openings are of two-ordered, recessed, Norman type, the only specifically Norman feature in any of these towers. They are merely a late group of western English Carolingian bell towers which have dropped some Saxon features and which show some Norman 'feeling'. It does not seem meaningful to classify these towers into a separate group. They are merely Saxon towers which show their late dates by certain minor modifications in their fabrics.

Axial towers

The term axial is used of two towers, a western and central, which lie on the main axis of a church, ie, in axial relationship with each other. It is also applied to a single tower, of the type to be described, which may be placed anywhere on the main axis of a non-cruciform church. Such towers are called axial towers. The ground floor forms part of the nave and the tower may be in any position, western, central or eastern; the exterior width is the same as that of the nave over a portion of which it stands: ie, it is integral with the nave and not just built against it. The walls are sometimes of the same thickness as the nave wall; in some the north and south walls are

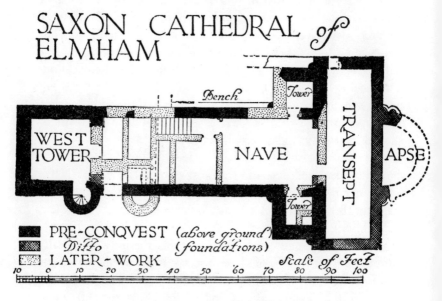

Fig 9. North Elmham Cathedral plan

thickened by a foot or so internally though flush with the nave walls outside. There is internal thickening of the walls at North Elmham (by about 18 in), Dunham Magna (by about 1 ft 9 in), at Tollesbury (by over 2 ft, nave walls about 3 ft, tower walls over 5 ft). There is only slight thickening at Swyncombe, and none at Castle Rising and Sompting.

Even when the tower is centrally placed, ie, at the east end of the nave, it is not a true central tower. The latter has connection with lateral north and south arms (porticus or transepts); it surmounts a crossing and has its own quoins to the ground, as at Breamore. An axial tower has no such connections; it occurs only in non-cruciform churches and its quoins do not extend below the top of the nave or chancel walls.

There are western axial towers at North Elmham (Norfolk) (fig 9), Tollesbury (Essex), Sompting (Sussex) (plates p 134); central ones at Dunham Magna (Norfolk), Langford and North Leigh (Oxon), Waithe (Lincs), probably at North Walsham (Norfolk), and at the overlap churches of Castle Rising chapel (Norfolk), and possibly Swyncombe (Oxon);[13] eastern ones, ie, over the west end of the chancel, are at Newton-by-Castle Acre and nearby Guestwick, and at Weybourne (Norfolk). There may formerly have been a western one at Northchurch (Herts) where there is an internal thickening of the west and south walls, about 25 ft along the south wall, which would give a tower of about 22 ft square.

Baldwin Brown regarded these towers 'as a Saxon form perpetuated in England in Norman times.' Certainly there are many post-Saxon ones. W. H. Godfrey[14] describes eleven axial towers of post-Saxon date in the county of Sussex alone, all in the eastern or central position. Among these are Kingston Buci, where a thirteenth century chancel and axial tower, of the same width as the nave, are built against an eleventh century Saxon nave; and at the early Norman (c 1120) church at Newhaven. Other western ones are at Diddlebury (Salop) and Hooton Pagnell near Doncaster, both post-Conquest.

Western annexes to western towers

At the west end of some churches are, or were, western annexes of unknown character; they may have been towers (as probably at South Elmham) or porches or narthexes, or sacristies of some kind. Whatever they were, they were axial with or without some thickening of the walls. One still exists up to about 14 ft at South Elmham (fig 10) where the thickening is about 8 in (nave 3 ft 10 in, annexe 4 ft 6 in). Others of

Fig 10. South Elmham, Old Minster plan

which there are some only slight monumental indications as they have long since been incorporated with the nave, were at Daglingworth (Glos) with a thickening of about 13 in, Boarhunt and Breamore (Hants) and Westdean (Sussex) with no thickenings. The annexe of West Dean was markedly rectangular, 16 ft 6 in by 7 ft; it was raised into a tower of the same unusual dimensions in the fourteenth century.

At Boarhunt the only indication is a slight tear-away on the nave south wall interior, the only remains of a wall dividing the nave into two portions, the western one being rectangular, about 14 ft E–W; the longer axis lies N–S. Perhaps the annexe at Northchurch was of this type, and not necessarily a tower.

Staircase towers

Staircase towers spread to England from Carolingian France, doubtless inspired by the now famous St Riquier (fig 1). They occur at the ruined North Elmham cathedral (fig 9), of unknown date but probably early eleventh century and certainly before 1075 when the See was transferred to Thetford. This was a typical cruciform Carolingian church with an apsidal chancel and eastern transept of tau form, ie, there was no presbyterial space between transept and apse. There were square towers in the re-entrant angles between transepts and nave, where staircase towers were usually situated in Carolingian churches. There are no certain remains of stairs in what is left of these towers and what evidence there is, is against their being staircase towers. They were more likely flanking towers for some other purpose: thus, their walls were thicker than those of nave or transepts, and they opened into nave and transepts. They or their ground floors may have been porticus. There was certainly a half-round staircase tower at the extreme east end of the south wall of the western tower.

There were staircases or staircase towers at Wilfrid's seventh century church at Hexham. Eddius refers to spiral stairs leading up and down, and Richard of Hexham, prior from 1142–74 (who may however have been referring to a later church) mentions round towers containing staircases for access to galleries. This was a century earlier than St Riquier, or Aachen. From where did Wilfrid get his inspiration? There is no record of staircase towers at St Martin at Tours, built 466–70. Wilfrid also knew Rome but there were none in Italy except staircases in walls at Sta Costanza, Rome, and S Lorenzo, Milan, both fourth century. The earliest staircase towers we know of where at St George, Salonica, c 400, in the later part of the church (the tower in the earlier part was Roman see above p 25), and at S Vitale, Ravenna, c 526–47.

Most other Saxon staircase towers were of the three-quarter-round type. There are four of these: at Brigstock (probably mid-eleventh century); Brixworth (fig 8) (third quarter of tenth century [Baldwin Brown], mid-eleventh, or even later, [Hamilton Thompson], very early ninth century, the most recent estimate [E. C. Gilbert]), both in Northants; Broughton-by-Brigg (later than the tower, but Saxon) and Hough-on-the-Hill (bonded into the tower and so presumably contemporary with it), both in Lincs. A peculiar spiral staircase is built into the north-east corner of the tower at Great Hale (Lincs) which is

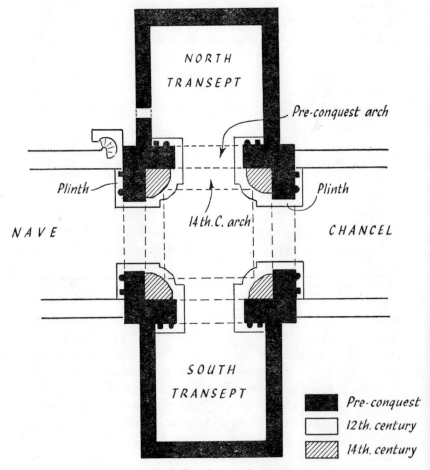

NORTH
TRANSEPT

Pre-conquest arch

Plinth

Plinth

NAVE

14th.C. arch

CHANCEL

SOUTH
TRANSEPT

■ Pre-conquest
□ 12th. century
▨ 14th. century

Fig 11. Stow (Lincs), central crossing plan

reminiscent of those at St George (Salonica) and S Lorenzo (Milan). These staircase towers are not all of identical type. Brigstock had a wooden staircase, long since destroyed and replaced by ladders.

Brixworth is unique in England. It is spiral, round a central column or newel of rubble, and has a continuous barrel vault of tufa, between the newel and the wall, spiralling up to near the top. The stone steps are set in mortar upon the back or upper surface of the vault. This is a very different construction from the Lincolnshire staircases. At Broughton the central newel is built up of drums. It is separate from the stairs which are fitted in between newel and wall.

At Great Hale the staircase is singularly small. It is of crude construction. Its central newel is 16 in in diameter and the stairs only 18 in wide. Even so, the corner thickening of the wall was not sufficient to contain it; the lower east face of the wall was built out in a somewhat bulging manner to accommodate it. It differs from the other English staircase towers in that the steps are not separated from the newel: ie, not wedged in between newel and wall. Each drum of the newel and its associated step is cut from one stone. According to H. M. and J. Taylor, this is a late feature met with in post-Conquest and medieval times and they consider the tower to be of post-Conquest and perhaps of genuinely medieval date. But the well-known Saxon chancel arch at Wittering (Northants), with its complicated soffit and face rolls and pilaster strips, is built up of drums in a similar way, each drum cut to complete profile shape. On this evidence, Wittering should be Norman or medieval too; few would agree with this!

There are square staircase towers of post-Conquest date at Weaverthorpe (Yorkshire, East Riding) at Stow (Lincs) (fig 11). and at Guestling (Sussex). At Weaverthorpe it is attached to the north-east corner of the tower and is contemporary with it, c 1110–20. The large rectangular one at Stow is now at the extreme north-east end of the nave, close to the north transept; it rises to well above the nave eaves and looks rather like a huge flat buttress. It is twelfth century work, contemporary with the nave. It was originally in the nave against the west face of the north-west crossing pier, ie, exactly on the inner side of the wall where it is now on the outer side.

At Guestling the square staircase tower is at the north-west corner of the west tower and has an internal newel staircase. It is contemporary with the western tower. The latter is not bonded into the nave wall and so may be of later date. The tower is similar to that at Bishopstone a few miles away. It is very Saxon looking, of tall slender proportions, of three stages with no string between the two lower stages though there is one below the third, or belfry, stage which is recessed. It is of doubtful date. Some authorities (V.C.H.) date the nave to the eleventh century and the tower to the early twelfth, perhaps as early as c 1100.

Adjuncts to western towers

These are best dealt with under towers as their functions are included in what may be called 'the tower system or complex'. There are few such adjuncts in this country and of these, only fragments or foundations remain. Some extended the entire length of the west end to form a narthex which was a characteristic of Byzantine churches. It was a kind of sub-church, usually of three laterally disposed compartments extending across the western end of the church, or in some circular or polygonal churches, such as S Vitale, across one of the corners. It was used for catechumens, candidates for baptism, or penitents. It is different from a porch although the central portion was often used as a porch. It spread later to the West and occurs in many basilican churches. Later, in the Gothic Period, it developed into the Galilee.

At Corbridge there are no indications of north or south adjuncts to the early porch, below the tower. Running for an undetermined distance west from the tower and in line with the north and south walls, foundations of walls were discovered. They may have been part of an atrium, or more likely a passage-way to some other building—possibly a monastery. The church was monastic but the monastery buildings were probably of wood and no traces remain.

At nearby Bywell St Peter's, foundations have been excavated which may have been part of an early narthex. They measure about 19 ft 6 in N–S, the same as the nave, by 11 ft 4 in E–W.

At Jarrow (plate p 35) the present chancel was originally the nave of an earlier church, smaller than and to the east of the main church, now replaced by the existing structure. Abbot Aldwine, c 1074, rebuilt the church and the tower connecting the two churches so that the nave of the eastern church became the chancel, separated by the tower which he built, from what remained of the ruined main church, the chancel of which he rebuilt as the nave of his new church. E. C. Gilbert,[15] in his careful study of the church and the literary evidence, suggested that a narthex probably extended across the entire width of the eastern church, and that traces of it are still recognisable in the lower part of the tower complex. It was probably two-staged. There were north and south narrow round-headed arches in the ground floor stage, but double-splayed (the only double-splayed openings in Northumbria) north and south windows in the second stage; there are signs of a door-way, long since blocked, in the east wall, near the south wall, through which the stage could be reached by ladder. Above the narthex, Abbot Aldwine erected his tower to cover the entire area of the narthex; this would explain the unusual shape of the tower (see p 50).

At Monkwearmouth, the Greenwell Committee in 1866 stated that they discovered foundations to north, south and west of the tower. Hall's excavations of 1924 confirmed the foundations to the west but failed to find any north and south. Recently Dr Rosemary Cramp of the Department of Archaeology, Durham University, has exposed the foundations of a wall running south for about 12 ft from the porch south wall.

It was about 2 ft wide and 7 ft 6 in from the junction of porch and nave and so set back, by perhaps 2 ft, from the porch west wall. At the south end of the wall, 'there appeared to be a junction with a feature both to west and east of the wall.' Owing to the very disturbed nature of the ground further excavations have, so far, failed to reveal remains to the east of the wall so there is no positive evidence that the wall was part of a porticus or narthex. It must have been part of some kind of annexe as suggested by the two-way junction at the south end.[16] The foundations to the west may have been part of a passage (as at Corbridge) leading to another building, either monastic, or another church. It is known that there were three churches on the site, all traces of the other two having disappeared. C. A. R. Radford, H. M. and J. Taylor and E. C. Gilbert[17] think there was a narthex across the west front, of which the existing two-staged original porch was the centre section forming, as it were, a short tower, the upper central stage of which was a chapel, ie, a Kaiserhalle, as at later Aachen.

At Brixworth, projecting north and south near the ground and pointing north and south, are two bits of walling, thinner than the walls (showing them to be contemporary). These are remains of western adjuncts of some kind, probably a narthex extending across the entire west end, the porch which may have been two-staged, being the centre of the complex. The original small north and south doorways in the tower ground floor, opened to the ground floors of the two adjuncts. There are no upper north and south doorways to communicate with upper stages of a narthex.

At Warblington (Hants) there are round-headed openings in the south, west and north walls of the tower second stage, the only stage now remaining. The north and south doorways must have been entrances to, presumably, the upper floors of two-staged north and south adjuncts, probably a narthex.

At Netheravon (Wilts) there were north, south and west adjuncts to the tower and three doorways in the tower at the same level. Remains of these three adjuncts are still visible in the tower walls; the ones at north and south had walls 9 ft apart and 2 ft thick, those at the west end are 10 ft 8 in apart and 2 ft thick. The western adjunct may have been a west-work as at Barton-on-Humber, the north and south ones porti-cus; the north one was probably two-staged for there is a doorway in the tower north wall about 17 ft above ground.

3 ROUND TOWERS

East Anglian round towers

These are essentially western bell towers but in some respects are so very different from the square ones, and so alike among themselves in general and often specific characteristics, that the phrase *sui generis* can be applied appropriately to them. They are characteristic of East Anglian church architecture for there are very few in England outside this area: only four and the foundations of four others in Essex, two in Cambridgeshire, one in Northants, two in Berkshire, one in Surrey and three (close together in and near Lewes) in Sussex. There are approximately 170 in East Anglia—129 in Norfolk and 41 (Cautley) or 42 (Morley) in Suffolk.

To what do these towers owe their peculiar shape? A main reason certainly is the absence of good building stone for quoins and dressings in this area. North and west of a line running north-south through Norwich to near Ipswich and then south-west, the area consists of chalk with abundant flints (very similar to parts of Sussex); to east and south of the line is alluvial clay. There is no building stone in the area and it was separated from the good oolitic country of Northants by forest and marshy fen with only poor roads and tracks and shallow rivers. The East Anglian builders had to use the local material available: usually flints from the chalk, pebbles including beach pebbles, sometimes pudding stone, a type of conglomerate. In other parts of the country, as in Sussex, where stone was scarce quoins were made of the same material as the walls, flints or rubble, sometimes specially selected for size and shape. In East Anglia the quoining difficulty was overcome by dispensing with corners and making the towers of circular section. Such towers, especially when they taper upwards as some

Page 71: Above: *(left)* Stow, W crossing arch from nave; *(right)* Sompting, tower arch and N capital and jamb. Below: *(left)* Haddiscoe, tower arch and upper doorway from nave; *(right)* Breamore, arch to S porticus.

do, are very strong, as is indicated by the great number which have out-lasted the churches to which they were attached.

It is difficult to date these towers. Some, eg, Bessingham, Colney, East Lexham, Haddiscoe, Roughton among others, are unquestionably Saxon in date and manner of building: some have double-splayed windows, and typical Saxon double belfry openings, sometimes gabled, and occuli (ie, circular windows). The great majority, however, have no specifically Saxon features and not always specifically Norman ones; these cannot be accepted or rejected as Saxon on this account; many openings originally cut through the walls, or left in them, were altered in post-Saxon times and often dressed with imported stone hiding their original character—as at Colney where the tall tower arch was described by J. Gunn[1] in 1849 as rough and primitive, of thin flints of a shape selected to best form an arch, with several pieces of rough stone as imposts. The present dressings, neo-Norman in appearance, were subsequent to 1849. Some, including some genuinely Saxon ones as at Haddiscoe (plates pp 53, 107), and nearby Herringfleet, have later belfry stages of apparently Norman form: at Haddiscoe the double openings are of Norman type, octagonal shafts with scalloped capitals and bases, instead of bulging balusters. These two also have much billet ornament, perhaps the earliest type of Norman ornament to be introduced into England and used, as here, in Anglo-Saxon settings.

Most writers, including J. C. Cox,[2] seem to think a majority are of post-Saxon date, with perhaps a few even post-Norman. The truth is that there are few features in these towers to justify definite attributions of Norman date, apart from some individual features present (as later additions) in some certainly Saxon towers. A sharp differentiation into those that are, and those that are not, Saxon would be difficult to justify, as the absence of any feature specifically Saxon does not definitely rule out a Saxon date. In some cases, eg, Little Saxham with its elaborate and beautiful late Norman ornament and particularly regular flint walling, the tower may be Norman throughout. At the

E

other end of the scale is Roughton with its rough walling and complete absence of stone dressings, and where the double belfry openings with mid-wall shafts and gabled heads are of flint: quite clearly an all-Saxon tower. In between are all the others, some with no Norman features, others with some, but most showing some features which are probably or possibly Saxon, or features which, according to the available evidence, are just as likely to be Saxon or Norman.

The difficulty of dating these towers may be illustrated by comparing the opinions of five well-known writers on Norfolk churches: J. C. Cox, Baldwin Brown, J. M. Cautley, H. M. and J. Tayor and A. B. Whittingham.[3] Cox gave a list of twenty-three which he considered to be certainly, probably, possibly, wholly or in part Saxon. In the body of his book he described five of his twenty-three as Norman, leaving eighteen as Saxon. Baldwin Brown deleted three from Cox's list and added two, making his list to number twenty-two. Cautley's list contained thirty-seven, and the Taylor's thirty. Sixteen of Cox's eighteen were common to all four lists. Great Ryburgh is in all four lists yet Whittingham wrote of it: 'It appears to me to belong to a group of early Norman work which exists in West Norfolk and probably had its origin in the early Norman work at Castle Acre. The tower arch is recessed in characteristic Norman manner, and there appears to me to be no feature in the tower which can definitely be put down as Saxon.' But nothing can be learnt from the dressings of openings in these towers; they are nearly all later, ie, post-Saxon, as at Colney.

The origin of round towers is obscure. Some early writers, eg, John Britton, attributed them to the Danes, a theory revived later by C. Morley. This is unlikely on two grounds: there are no such towers in neighbouring Lincolnshire or anywhere else in Danish England north of the Humber, nor are there any in Denmark, Norway, Sweden or the valley of the Elbe. Moreover the Danish and Scandinavian building traditions, like the original Anglo-Saxon, were in timber. Christianity spread to Norway from England c 950, the Norwegian church being set up c 995 from England, but stone building was not begun there till c 1100. Denmark appears to have been influenced from Germany for it was in the ecclesiastical province of Hamburg-Bremen from c 950 to 1103; stone building began there c 1050, ie, at about the same time as Norman-Romanesque began to show itself in England. Both these dates are later than the earliest round towers of East Anglia.

The Danish invaders were dominant in East Anglia, as later the Normans were dominant throughout England. If, as is of course very probable and perhaps certain for they became Christians, the Danes founded churches in their settlements, it is more than likely that Saxon masons would have done the building.

S. E. Rigold[4] has suggested that the great majority of these towers, though not all pre-Conquest, are essentially Saxon, or, as he prefers to express it, more generally, *premier roman* or First Romanesque in style; ie, that they are a local East Anglian variety of that First Romanesque style which developed in Lombardy in the mid-ninth century and spread westwards. He thinks the towers were built as attached western bell towers in the century between c 1015 and c 1115, and that the style was not affected significantly by the Norman Conquest. It is known that the First Romanesque style spread to French and Spanish Catalonia and Andorra by the mid-tenth century, and up the valleys of the Rhone and Saone. According to Clapham,[5] it spread to some degree to Switzerland and 'thence in isolated examples into Germany and the Low Countries. . . . There is no evidence that it passed the watershed of the Rhone and the Loire. . . . Elsewhere in north and north-west France it is entirely unrepresented.' Rigold's theory is plausible, but round towers were not a feature of the First Romanesque style. Moreover, as stated above, the earliest round bell towers were at Ravenna after 973, a century later than the beginning of the First Romanesque; they could not have passed west with, or in the wake of, the First Romanesque.

It seems more likely that we owe round towers to that

Carolingian influence which emanated from St Riquier. The St Riquier towers were staircase towers and crossing towers; the East Anglian towers were neither. But the circular shape of the former may have impressed East Anglian masons as being a simple method of avoiding quoining.

Some writers, eg, H. M. Cautley, consider that these towers were built as defence or refuge towers and that the churches were built later against the towers. This is extremely unlikely. They were small, some not more than eight or ten feet across. Many had no exterior doorways (as at Bessingham, Colney, East Lexham, Roughton), nor indeed any exterior openings at all (Bessingham, Colney). There was often a doorway of ingress to the second stage in the east wall above the tower arch and which could be reached by ladder from the nave (at Bessingham, Haddiscoe [plate p 71], Roughton). But the churches were thatched as many are today, so the tower would be vulnerable to fire unless the ground stage was vaulted— and none were. There were no interior stairs so ladders were used for access to the upper stages as they are today.

In many cases it is clear that the tower was built against an existing church, or was contemporary with it, for the lower east faces of some are more or less flat to make attachment to the nave easier, eg, at Bessingham. In many, though by no means all, there are flint fillings, three-quarter-round angle shafts between the tower and nave west wall (as at Colney, Haddiscoe and Witton); in some, the outer face of the filling is plane, in others segmental with the convexity (as at Roughton, plate p 53) facing outwards. The later quarter- and half-round flint pilaster strips round the apse at North Elmham clearly belong to the same tradition.

These towers range in internal diameter from 8 ft to 20 ft, the walls from 2 ft 6 in to 6 ft in thickness, and in height from approximately 35 ft to 60 ft. Some have two or three string courses corresponding to three or four internal stages (Haddiscoe); others have no strings (Bessingham, Colney, East Lexham, Roughton).

Irish round towers

These were, and still are, as striking a feature of the land-
scape as spires are in England. They differ from the East
Anglian round towers in appearance and function. They are
free-standing, not attached to churches. All were monastic,
ie, they were built by monks within monastic precincts and
usually near the church or chapel. They were built originally
as belfries (their Irish name is *cloictech*—bell-house) but they
were also watch towers and refuges for the monks and their
treasures during raids—of barbarians from overseas and no
doubt also from Irish raiders, for Ireland was by no means a
settled and peaceful country in the centuries of these towers.

They were not staircase towers[6] like those attached to
churches. Access to their upper floors was by removable ladders.
Floors were usually of timber. They were singularly attractive
in appearance: relatively very tall and slender (height to
breadth ratios of about one to six; those for East Anglian round
towers were one to two or three), tapering markedly upwards
and surmounted by stone roofs—tallish, pointed and conical,
made by corbelling (plate p 17). The only entrance was 10 ft to
15 ft above the ground, reached by a ladder which could be
pulled up by the defenders and the door closed. A port nearby
made it possible to overturn the ladders of attackers. Each
stage had one small, narrow, loop window, these so arranged
that each commanded a different aspect so that stones and
missiles could be thrown against attackers from all sides.
Immediately below the cap was usually a range of four windows,
enabling a look-out to be kept in all directions. Many openings
were gable-headed, others had flat or arched lintels, all were
single-splayed. The towers were built of mortared stone but on
shallow foundations; many have collapsed, some now diverge
from the perpendicular. The earlier ones (eg, at Castledermot)
are of rather rough, primitive work in unworked stone or
rubble. Later ones such as the twelfth century one at Ardmore,
co Waterford[7] are of fine ashlar. The Ardmore tower is of

blocks carefully cut not only to the curve of the wall, but according to de Paor, to supply an entasis.

Although the great majority of Irish round towers are free-standing, a few are attached to churches as belfries. Among these are St Kevin's Church, Glendalough, co Wicklow[8] where the short, slender tower rests on the west gable. The church is possibly ninth century but the tower is later, though possibly not much later. Another is Trinity church, Glendalough, where the tower, now collapsed, rested on the walls of a square western annexe, both of later date than the church which may well be of the tenth century. The annexe is not a porch as there is no exterior opening; the only entrance is from the nave.

These two towers, though somewhat later than the churches, are among the earliest of the group. This supports the view that such towers were first introduced as attached belfries (de Paor). Later when the Viking raids became more frequent and calamitous, the need for refuge for monks and their treasure led to the erection of the much larger and taller and more elaborate free-standing towers which, usually close to the church, could still serve as belfries.

F. Henry is of the opinion that attached, round belfry towers date generally from the twelfth century. Neither de Paor nor Henry gives evidence supporting the dates but on general grounds de Paor's dating would appear to be the more likely.

De Paor states that there is or was a small round tower attached to the gable end of the little church on Lambay Island off the Dublin coast. This island was the scene of the first Viking raid of 795. The tower of St Finghan's church, Clonmacnoise, co Offaly[9] is at the south-east corner of the nave, overlapping the chancel; its only access is from the chancel. It rises from the ground (unlike the two at Glendalough) 48 ft to the cap and 56 ft to the cap apex. The date is probably c 1160–70 and so belongs to the Irish Romanesque period.

Baldwin Brown and Conant think the towers date back to the Carolingian age: the Viking raids began in 795. This would preclude any derivation from Eastern-Ravennate models of free-standing, round bell towers, the earliest of which was after 850 (see p 185).[13] But none survive of earlier date than the tenth century. De Paor thinks that though the idea of the tower was almost certainly suggested by foreign belfries, the form was clearly developed in Ireland. It is found in every part of the country but is rare elsewhere; there are two in Scotland at Abernethy and Brechin, and one in the Isle of Man. At Abernethy, a window near the cap has a deeply projecting, semi-circular hood mould and, below plain imposts, vertical pilaster strips alongside the jambs. This feature is clearly of Anglo-Saxon, not Irish, inspiration; it does not occur in Irish towers. A rather similar feature at Aghowle (co Wicklow) church—not tower—of early Romanesque date, is stated by Leask[10] to be unique in Ireland. Conant is of the opinion that they represent a 'basically northern design'. It would seem likely that the inspiration came from the St Riquier area, especially in view of the continuous intercourse between the monasteries of Ireland and of the west and north-west of Europe. Many monasteries abroad were Irish foundations (eg, those at Annegray, Luxeuel, St Gall and Bobbio were founded between 591 and 615 by the Irish monk, Columbanus, or his followers), filled largely with Irish monks, between whom and those at home were frequent interchanges.

But it may still be asked: why were these towers round in a country where, unlike East Anglia, there is an abundance of stone? Baldwin Brown suggested that 'ease of construction . . . may have conditioned the round form of plan.' There may perhaps be an additional factor operating as a pre-disposing cause of the form of these towers, viz, folk memory.

The primitive habitations of early man over wide areas were circular huts or shelters of reeds, and/or skins and other materials, with roofs of roughly conical, or even more roughly domical, shape. This type of shelter existed for centuries, perhaps millennia, before timber, or mud-brick, or stone was used as building material. This domical shape, together with the circular shape supporting it, would gradually become consciously appreciated as a shape, and later this consciousness of a shape would develop into the idea of a shape, or rather of two shapes comprised in the wider idea of a habitation. This would in due course become enlarged into the more complicated idea of a circular tribal or ancestral shelter and would acquire some religious significance. Baldwin Smith,[11] with a wealth of learning and many examples and illustrations, argues that the dome did not originate as a functional architectural feature but as an idea, as indicated above; ie, that a domical ideology preceded the architectural idea of a dome.

The domical idea persisted, even took a grip on the imagination of men, when more substantial buildings were erected, especially those of a religious character. Among the earliest of these were the *tholoi*—sacred shrines—built of pisé or clay on a circular plan and resting on foundations of rough stones, river boulders, pebbles and such like, discovered by M. E. L. Mallowan,[12] at Arpachiyah, a few miles east of Nineveh, and dated by him to perhaps very early in the fifth millennium BC. Such buildings spread westwards at least as far as Sicily and Etruscan Italy, the best known being the famous so-called treasury (but really the tomb chamber) of Atreus at Mycenae[13] dated possibly to the twelfth century BC. This type of building spread to Egypt and elsewhere in the early Middle East; it was constructed of oversailing courses of horizontal masonry with their ends shaped so as to give a continuous curve (this type of construction was later called 'corbelling out'), ending in a pointed top. This oversailing construction was not arch construction vertically and so was not a true dome in the modern sense of the word: it was of a domical shape, a variant of the earliest domical shapes out of which the modern dome developed. These buildings all had a religious significance, eg, tombs, tomb chambers and, in the early Christian period, mausolea, martyria and baptisteries.

Although the domical shape, sometimes from the ground upwards like the early *tholoi*, has persisted in hut design in many primitive areas[14] to the present day, it is the specifically religious building that is most closely associated with the word dome. Originally meaning a house or roof, only later a cupola, in the Middle Ages it came to mean any important house, and then a sacred house *(domus dei)*. Today we have the German *dom* and the Italian *duomo* meaning cathedral.

During the centuries of the migrations of peoples (say c AD 400 to 800), the wanderers reached Ireland, on the edge of the then known world, and there they developed a civilization which later became Christian and highly cultured. However, as in early Saxon England, it was technologically backward. Christopher Dawson[15] wrote that 'on the material side Anglo-Saxon civilization was a failure; its chief industry seems to have been the manufacture and export of saints.' This applies no less to Ireland.

Later contacts were with Northumbria and, through interchange of monks and scholars, a more or less unified artistic culture arose in those areas usually called the Hiberno-Saxon.[16] The influence of Irish culture, and later that of the Anglo-Saxons, was immense in western and north-western Europe owing to their amazing missionary activities.[17] During these close missionary contacts abroad, the Irish monks must have become familiar with towers, both square and round, and it seems not unreasonable to suppose that when the need for defence and refuge towers arose, the folk memories of the round domed habitations, the ancestral houses of ancient times, would as it were 'seep' to the surface and operate as a pre-disposing factor in favour of the circular shape and conical cap.

This influence of folk memory is by no means an illusion. It was not confined to architecture. It was operative also in the field of literature and general culture. The Christian culture which developed in Ireland and which made Ireland the leader of Western culture in the seventh century, owed much to ancient Irish tradition and this influence of tradition enabled the Irish monastic schools to replace the old druidic and bardic schools as the leaders of Irish society. Christopher Dawson[18] writes in connection with Ireland 'there can be no doubt that

. . . the literary tradition has its roots deep in the prehistoric past. The most striking example of this is the great prose epic or saga—the *Tain Bo Cualgne*—which takes us back . . . to the heroic age of Celtic culture and preserves the memory of a stage of society resembling that of the Homeric world.'

It was also undoubtedly a formative factor in the development of that fascinatingly beautiful Irish book illumination which reached its peak in the Book of Kells. Dr Françoise Henry[19] writes:

> We will perhaps never be able to assess how much survives . . . of very ancient prehistoric beliefs, and to what extent the [Irish] artist . . . is the successor to the magician, master of beings and of natural forces, who is his distant ancestor. But Irish epic poetry in which the mainspring of action is provided rather by geasa-magical interdictions—than by psychological reactions, introduces us probably to a world familiar to the artist. On these ancient data, elaborated into a reasoned discipline far removed from the dark influence of the primitive, was built up an artistic system at once subtle, coherent and harmonious in its strangeness, and this labyrinthine dream, this disciplined effervescence of the imagination, has never ceased to haunt and to trouble those who, in the course of the centuries, have met them face to face.

According to Conant, 118 towers exist in Ireland including thirteen in fairly perfect condition. De Paor states that about eighty survive in whole or in part. They vary in height from 60–120 ft.

They may have spread to some degree to the Celtic south-west of England. This is not surprising. Many Irish hermits settled in this area, as perhaps is indicated by the considerable number of church dedications to otherwise unknown Irish saints; many Irish missionaries too would sojourn temporarily here on their way to north-west Europe.[20] It is significant that Malmesbury Abbey (Wilts) and Glastonbury Abbey (Somerset) were Celtic foundations.

The old church of St Michael at East Teignmouth (fig 12), undoubtedly at least in part a Saxon one, was destroyed in

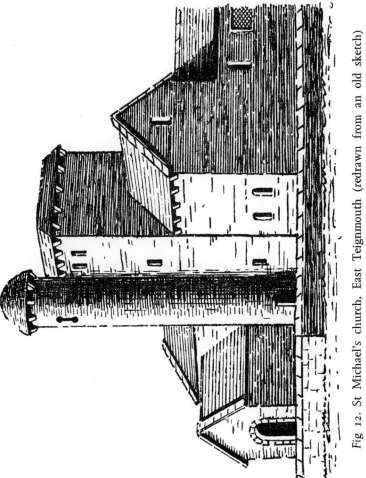

Fig 12. St Michael's church, East Teignmouth (redrawn from an old sketch)

1811 as it was too small to meet the needs of an increasing congregation. A contemporary sketch gives an impression of its general appearance. The circular stair tower attached to the south-west corner of the tower and extending well above the tower roof was strikingly Irish in appearance. There was a rectangular doorway at the base and a narrow loop window near the roof, which was of low mushroom or rounded conical shape.

There was a similar stair tower at the south-east corner of the tower of nearby Bishopsteignton, destroyed about the same time.[21]

4 OTHER TOWERS AND THEIR USES

Fortified or defence towers

It is not possible to say whether, or to what extent, towers were built in England specifically for defence purposes. There must have been some, especially north of the Humber and/or Tees, as protection during the innumerable Border raids from Scotland which extended over many centuries. The so-called Vicar's Pele at Corbridge, not attached to any church, is clearly a fortified tower dated to c 1300 and so outside our period. The great stone castles are also outside our period. Moreover we are concerned only with church towers used as refuges or for defence. The unlikelihood of East Anglian round towers being used for this purpose has been discussed above (p 76). Similar considerations apply to all church towers: they were vulnerable to fire unless the ground floor was vaulted which few, if any, were in Saxon days. An exception was Monkwearmouth where the ground floor (the original late-seventh century porch) was vaulted later, but not much later and in the Saxon period. It is the earliest vault above ground in England. Why was it vaulted? It was perhaps intended to increase the safety of the tower as a refuge; the second stage could be entered from the nave through the opening about 14 ft above the nave floor. This was in fact a window, probably not glazed, and so could be used as an entrance.

Some western towers, especially in Northumbria, had no external openings in the ground floor but with either a narrow doorway or wider arch leading to the nave; as at Billingham, Bywell St Andrews, Ingram, Ovingham, Morland, Skipwith, Monk Fryston, Whittingham, all north of the Humber, and Great Hale and Syston (Lincs), Carlton-in-Lindrick (Notts), Lavenden (Bucks), Caversfield (Oxon), Sompting (Sussex). With these too there would be fire hazards for the ground floors were not vaulted.

The only tower showing some evidence of defence intent is is that at Wickham (Berks) (plate p 133). Here the only external doorway, now blocked, is in the south wall about 8 ft above ground. The certainly ancient nave appears to have been built against the tower with a straight joint which indicates that the tower was built first, possibly as a free-standing refuge tower. However, the three lower stages, the top one being the belfry with the usual double openings, are contemporary with the ground floor. So the tower may originally have been a belfry-cum-defence tower.

The idea of using church towers as refuges was certainly not foreign to the Saxons. This seems evident from the existence of such towers in south Pembrokeshire in the early twelfth century (and so just outside our period). This small area, south of a line E–W through Haverfordwest and Narberth, was settled in 1107 by Flemings, largely from East Anglia. This area is still called 'Little England beyond Wales' and is English-speaking, in sharp contrast to the Welsh-speaking natives to the north of this line. Sir Thomas Jackson[1] wrote of these 'quaint little Pembrokeshire churches with their military looking towers, vaulted in the ground-story and furnished with pigeon holes in the upper stages, in which the villagers could take refuge . . . when the wild Welshmen made a raid into the English pale. Many of them are covered with barrel vaults from end to end, which form the exterior roof as well, without any timber at all.'

Dimensions of western towers

Though tall, slender proportions are characteristic of Saxon towers, the actual dimensions, and the relations between them, vary greatly from tower to tower. Dimensions are available, though not always complete, for over ninety towers from which it appears that heights vary from about 30 ft to 72 ft, and the average exterior wall breadth from 9 ft at Warblington

(Hants) to 26 ft at York. Average here means the sum of the north-south and east-west exterior widths divided by two. The mean height is about 55 ft which is also the modal height, ie, there are as many heights below as above this mean. This is significant as it suggests a random, ie, a fortuitous or accidental distribution of heights around a modal value. If, for example, there had been regional preferences for higher or lower towers, or for more or less slender proportions, it might be expected that such preferences would show themselves in more or fewer heights above or below the mean or mode. About sixty per cent are between 50 ft and 65 ft inclusive; of the remainder, about one-third are above 65 ft and two-thirds below 50 ft. Of mean wall breadths, the average is 18 ft 6 in, which is also modal.

Amidst this variety, the best indication of the slender proportions is perhaps the ratio height to mean exterior wall breadth : the mean value is 3 : 1; it varies from 1·6 to 4·25 to one. This range of variation is not affected markedly by tower height. Thus height ranges:

less than 50 ft	ratios are 1·6 to 3·1
between 50 ft and 65 ft	2·3 to 4·25
above 65 ft	2·8 to 4·0

Thurlby (Lincs) with a ratio of 1·6 : 1 has a height of only 30 ft and a wall width of 19 ft: it looks very Norman but its thin walls (3 ft 3 ins) and other features proclaim it to be Saxon. Singleton (Sussex) with a ratio of 2·25 : 1 looks very Norman, almost fortresslike due probably to the almost total lack of openings in the west wall (only one), no belfry openings and a single string course. Little Bardfield (Essex) (plate p 135), and Branston (Lincs) with almost identical ratios (2·3 : 1) look much less Norman due, respectively, to the numerous narrow openings (including belfry ones) and three strings; and one string and large belfry openings. Wall pilaster decorations, as at Barnack and Earls Barton (Northants), and many openings increase the apparent slenderness.

Wall thicknesses are also very variable. They range from 2 ft to 4 ft 6 in, the mean being 3 ft. Six have walls less than 2 ft 6 in thick and these are mostly of the same thickness as the nave walls: Kirk Hammerton (Yorks, West Riding) 2 ft 2 in–2 ft 11 in; Hainton (Lincs) 2 ft; Whittingham 2 ft 3 in–2 ft 6 in; Sompting (Sussex), Warblington (Hants) and Wootton Wawen (Warwicks) all 2 ft 3 in. Four are above 4 ft: Morland (Westmorland) 4 ft–4 ft 9 in; Great Hale (Lincs) about 4 ft 6 in; North Leigh (Oxon) about 4 ft 4 in; and Caistor (Lincs) 3 ft 8 in (south wall), 3 ft 10 in (west), 4 ft 11 in (north) and 5 ft 9 in–5 ft 11 in (east).

Some other ecclesiological uses of towers

A typical tower should have three stages, at least on the interior though not always indicated on the exterior by string courses. Of these, the top stage would be the belfry, the second stage the ringing chamber and the ground floor a porticus ingressus (or porch) or, if no external entrances, a porticus. Such a porticus might be used as a vestry or tomb chamber or might have a subsidiary altar. In one tower, Barnack, where in fact there is a south doorway, the ground floor is puzzling. In the centre of the interior west wall is a gable-headed recess obviously intended as a seat. During restoration work in 1854–5 traces of wooden seats sufficient for forty people were discovered, on either side of the central stone seat. On the north and south walls, near the tower arch and four feet above floor level, are small recesses resembling aumbries. Baldwin Brown gave his considered opinion that this porticus was not only used, but designed, for judicial purposes, the central seat being the judge's seat. He pointed out that parts of other churches were often so used even when, as in the north and south porch towers of Canterbury Cathedral, there were altars.

This explanation is far from convincing. Village churches in early times, especially of the non-monastic type, were used for many purposes other than religious ones. They were the social centres of the villages: fairs, markets, social gatherings, even

Page 89: (left) Brixworth, tower and staircase tower from S; (right) Barnack, tower from S.

Page 90: Above: Earls Barton: *(left)* top two stages of tower from S; *(right)* middle section of tower S wall, banded balusters. Below: *(left)* Barnack, tower arch from E; *(right)* Cambridge, St Benet's, belfry stage.

dances were held in them, ie, the naves. Certainly judicial
business was transacted somewhere in some of them and it was
unnecessary for them to be designed specially for such a purpose, especially on the scale of Barnack. It would seem to be
most unlikely for any such idea to be in the minds of the
builders of this tower. Clapham, wisely perhaps, is silent on the
problem. Talbot Rice makes the more likely suggestion that
the aumbry-like recesses really were aumbries, that there was an
altar in front of the central seat, and that the tower ground floor
was in effect a western apse, though square instead of round.
Western apses as well as eastern ones were a Carolingian feature.
Though there are references in contemporary literature to
double-apsed churches in Saxon England they were even less
popular than eastern ones. In some cases the English preference
for a fine western portal, made them substitute for a western
apse a gallery with altar raised on the nave west wall—as at
Deerhurst, Tredington and elsewhere—or go without a western
altar altogether or, as Talbot Rice suggests, to have an altar in
the tower ground floor with a south instead of a western portal.

Where there are more than three stages to a tower, the additional stages must have been built for special purposes; it is most
unlikely that they would have been inserted for decorative
reasons, eg, to produce towers of tall slender proportions and so
aesthetically attractive. It seems likely that the second stage,
immediately above the ground floor, was intended for a habitation, perhaps for a sacristan whose job it would be to care for
the treasures of the church, for bell-ringing, and to keep watch
over the altar to prevent theft and so on. It would be convenient,
in fact necessary, for him to live in the tower. This seems to have
been the case at Bosham (Sussex) and Deerhurst (Glos). At
Bosham (plate p 135), there is a gable-headed doorway in the
east wall about 18 ft above nave floor level, and to the south of
this a small rectangular window or squint. There was a gallery
(removed in the mid-nineteenth century) across the west end of
the nave. The doorway, reached presumably by ladder from the
interior ground floor, would give access to this gallery. The

F

squint would enable the inhabitant to keep, especially at night, watch on the altar. At Deerhurst (plate p 54) the arrangement is similar: a round-headed doorway about 16 ft above the floor with a small triangular squint to the south. The gallery has long since disappeared but stone brackets in the north and south walls, close to the west wall, were probably part of the gallery supports. There was probably a gallery at Brixworth; here however there was a large round-headed doorway, now blocked, leading to or from the second stage of the tower, but no squint. There is also plain evidence of a western gallery at Tredington (Worcs). H. M. Taylor thinks there was one at Jarrow entered through a doorway in the nave south wall; there are two blocked openings in the tower south wall. There was also a gallery at Wing (Bucks) but no tower.

At Monkwearmouth the second stage of the porch, entered by an opening from the nave about 14 ft above floor level, may have been occupied by a sacristan, as well as perhaps used as a refuge. E. C. Gilbert however gives some evidence that there may have been an altar here near the west end of the north-wall—an unusual position. It seems unlikely that an altar would be provided for a mere sacristan. There is much that is puzzling about this tower. In the present fourth stage, which normally would be the ringing chamber, is a blocked eastern doorway visible from the nave, at about 26 ft above the floor, and beside this, marks in the wall which might indicate the presence of a squint (now blocked) or of an altar, as possibly at Skipwith (Yorks). This stage also may have been inhabited: by a sacristan if there was a squint or by some more important person if there was an altar there. At Skipwith, in the interior east wall of the second internal stage of the tower, there is a shallow recess[2] 3 ft high by 3 ft 6 in wide and 6 in deep, and a sill about 2 ft above the present timber floor. It is lighted by a small window close to the east end of the south wall with its sill a little below the recess lintel. The use of this recess is not known. It is certainly later than the tower so must have had a special purpose. It seems too shallow to hold ornaments or relics, unless perhaps, as

Baldwin Brown suggested, they were reliefs like those in Chichester Cathedral; however, it seems unlikely that carvings would be hidden from general view in a specially made recess high up in the tower. It is not recognisably an altar site and there is no evidence of an altar here. It is, however, consistent with being a background or reredos of an altar and the idea is tempting. If an altar, this stage may have been inhabited by someone more important than a sacristan, but there is no indication of an opening in the east wall so the occupier could not see the main altar or follow the services.

At Deerhurst in the third stage of the tower is the well known massive gable-headed double opening in the east wall overlooking the nave, its sill about 28 ft above the nave floor (plate p 108). E. C. Gilbert thinks this stage is of later date than the ones below and was built specifically as a chapel. This might seem unlikely for chapels in towers were almost unknown in western Europe. It is true there were chapels in the top stages of the three western staircase towers at St Riquier, and apparently also at St Gall (say c 790–820), but no others are known of that date. On the other hand, Charlemagne built a chamber above the central portion of the ambulatory of his palace chapel at Aachen so that he could follow the services in private. It is not unlikely that there may have been an altar there to serve for his own family worship.

Offa, the great king of Mercia, was a monarch of considerable importance in western Europe; he corresponded with Charlemagne on terms of equality. He might, not unnaturally, have wished to copy his greater contemporary by having a similar arrangement at his cathedral at Lichfield, which he made an archiepiscopal church for some years, or perhaps at Repton which was more closely associated with the royal family. There is no evidence for this, but if he did so, some of his more important ealdormen might copy him and have their own private apartments, possibly with altars, in the churches which they built and frequented, or to which they gave gifts or endowments. Both Brixworth and Deerhurst were monastic and the local ealdormen or thegns may well have been generous in their gifts and been granted the special privileges of private chapels in the towers. It may be relevant that the openings in these stages at Brixworth and Deerhurst, double at Deerhurst and triple at Brixworth, are elaborately ornamented which suggests that the occupiers were people of importance.

There are openings of simpler design at higher levels at Bosham, east face at 29 ft; Lincoln (St Mary-le-Wigford and St Peter-at-Gowts) at 26 ft; at Earls Barton at 25 ft. It is thought by most writers that these openings were ingresses to inter-roof spaces. Such were known in some native Irish churches. At Earls Barton the opening is above the present nave roof but was originally below the external nave roof. At Deerhurst there is one very high up, about 40 ft, in the east wall of the fourth stage and now partly above the nave modern roof. Other examples are at Ovingham (at 27 ft up), probably Bywell (Northumberland), Jarrow, possibly Billingham (co Durham), Burghwallis, Skipwith, Weaverthorpe, Wharram-le-Street, possibly Middleton-by-Pickering (Yorks), Barton-on-Humber (here there are two, leading formerly to chambers respectively above the original chancel and now below the roof of the later nave, from which it is visible, and above the western annexe), Hough-on-the-Hill, Marton, Nettleton, Scartho, Thurlby, Winterton, (all Lincs), Brigstock and Barnack (at the latter about 35 ft up, above the present nave ceiling and below the marks of the original roof on the tower east wall), Repton (Derbys), St Benet's, Cambridge, Clapham and St Peter de Merton (Bedford), Lavendon (Bucks), Langford (Oxon) on the west face only of this central axial tower, Bessingham, Haddiscoe (plate p 71), Roughton round towers (Norfolk), Singleton and Sompting (Sussex) at 29 ft. They also occur in a few central towers: at Norton, one in each of the four wall faces, and at Dover (St Mary in Castro), in the west face only above the western arch.

5 BELFRIES

A belfry is that stage of a tower in which the bell or bells are hung. It is usually, though not always, the top stage, the one below being the ringing chamber. In some cases the original Saxon belfry has been rebuilt or replaced by one of later date, Norman or post-Norman. Occasionally a new and additional stage has been added as a belfry, in which case it is generally plain that the original belfry was the stage below, as at Alkborough, Barton-on-Humber, Bosham, Monk Fryston, Wickham, and perhaps Skipwith and Barnack.

Belfry openings

Belfry openings are frequently called windows. They were so called by Baldwin Brown and other writers, but are not. All Saxon windows are single or double splayed; belfry openings, like the very great majority of doorways, are cut straight through the wall. Belfry openings are neither windows nor doorways; they are sound holes and should be called 'belfry openings'.

They are generally double and rectangular in shape. Each half is covered with a round arch, the two central meeting ends of which would, as it were, hang in the air if they were not supported from below by a mid-wall shaft—round, square, polygonal, or rectangular with rounded edges—or in, perhaps, earlier types bulging baluster shafts. Between the shaft and the arch head is a rectangular through-stone the length of the wall thickness (hence its name). This holds up the arch and is itself supported by the shaft beneath. The jambs are normally of throughstones, two or more to each jamb in vertical arrangement, and there are square-edged square or rectangular imposts above the jambs, corresponding to the impost above the mid-wall shaft; there may also be similarly square-edged bases or plinths to both jambs and shafts. This fundamental simple type appears in a variety of forms; some differences are slight, others sufficient to throw light on dating problems.

The arch heads may be cut: from one high flat lintel stone, ie, two apparent arch heads from a single stone; from two half-length, laterally disposed, lintel stones to provide two apparent arches, one to each half opening; arch heads may be cut from both the upper and lower faces of the stone or stones. The first two types may be called 'arched lintels', and the third type, 'double arched lintels'. They are not of course arches at all, their thrust being entirely vertically downwards, as with flat lintels.

Though account must be taken of local variations and pre-ferences, and of differing rates of development in different districts, it may be stated broadly that arched lintels are the earliest type of belfry-opening head, single-arched lintels being perhaps earlier than the double-arched type, ie, typologically if not chronologically. A few (such as East Lexham, Norfolk) have heads and jambs of rough rubble work. These may be regarded as the earliest type typologically but not chronologically. There may be special reasons for such primitiveness, such as lack of stone, especially in East Anglia. These are indeed relatively very numerous. Among them are: Billingham, Bolam (double), Bywell St Andrews (double), Corbridge, Jarrow upper belfry (double), Monkwearmouth, Ovingham, Appleton-le-Street, Wharram-le-Street, Kirk Hammerton, Monk Fryston, Cambridge St Benet's (here the arched lintel does not go far into the wall; behind is a roughly made rere arch of rubble), Earls Barton (a quintuple opening of double-arched lintels—plate p 90), Carlton-in-Lind-rick, North Leigh, Barton-on-Humber (second stage, not belfry, double), Clee, Marton (double), Rothwell (double), Scartho (double), Syston (double), Waithe, Winterton.

Another early development was the attempt to form crude arch heads. Thus, some arch heads are of rubble stones cut roughly to shape and to different lengths, or may be just selected as suitable. Such rough heads are at Hovingham and Tredington (of thin rubble slabs badly arranged), Oxford St Michael's, Lavendon and East Lexham. Others of rather more advanced character are made of very few stones of varying lengths, cut to length and to the appropriate curved shape; among these are Burghwallis, a blocked doorway in Bracebridge nave, and the transept arches at Norton. This arrangement is often met with in larger arches (as at Norton), but is rare in belfries, partly because with such small arches it was easier to make them gable-headed, as at: Barton-on-Humber (third stage, original belfry—plate p 35), Bessingham, Haddiscoe (plate p 53), Roughton, Newton-by-Castle Acre (gabled with Roman bricks, oversailing in stepped pattern), Sompting (four single gabled—two in each east and west wall, four pairs of double-gabled—two pairs in each north and south wall, all in stone with rounded front edges —plates p 134).

Genuine voussoired heads are at Jarrow (third stage, early belfry), Bardsey, York, Alkborough, Barton-on-Humber (fourth stage, post-Conquest), Bracebridge, Branston, Glentworth, Lincoln (St Mary-le-Wigford and St Peter-at-Gowts), Bosham (plate p 135), Singleton, Wickham and Winterton. At Colchester the heads are turned in Roman bricks. In some very late post-Conquest belfries, the heads are not only of well cut regular voussoirs but the heads and central imposts are thinner than the tower wall; ie, they are recessed in Norman manner within a single round head of voussoirs in the outer wall. Examples are at Weaverthorpe and Clapham. Both are of very early twelfth century date; some writers consider them to be Norman; but they have few, if any, Norman features. In manner of building they seem more Saxon than Norman. This type in its fully developed form also occurs, of course, in all genuine Norman belfries built above Saxon belfries or as replacements of original Saxon belfries. Examples are at Middleton-by-Pickering, Wickham (plate p 133) and, perhaps, Langford.

Some other variations are worthy of note. In a few belfries one of the four openings is single, contrasting with the three double openings. Among these is Bardsey: here the eastern openings of the belfry, and of the stage below, are narrow single openings with arched lintels, contrasting with the voussoired double openings of the south wall of both stages. H. M. Taylor considers these two single openings to represent a type of belfry opening earlier, chronologically and typologically, than the more familiar and complicated double openings. The latter are too complex to have arisen suddenly; they almost presuppose a preliminary period of development. Here, at Bardsey, Taylor thinks we may have, on adjacent walls, the familiar double openings and a precursor, both of contemporary date. It may well be that the single type was the earlier, and that the double type, so clearly liked by the Saxon, was substituted for it later. No intermediate forms are known, though as shown above, many variations developed.

At Skipwith (plate p 18), in the fourth stage—the one below the fifteenth-century belfry—are four small rectangular openings in the blockings of larger round-headed openings which Taylor regards as the original belfry single openings, although there is no evidence that this very short stage was a belfry; the stage below, also low, would have been the ringing chamber but it has no openings. A completely dark ringing chamber is not easy to accept. Baldwin Brown surmised that the present fifteenth-century belfry may have replaced a Saxon belfry, or part of it. There is no evidence for this either, but it may well be true. In this case the stage below, with the large single windows, would have been the ringing chamber.

Mid-Wall columns and bulging balusters

Characteristic of double openings is the mid-wall shaft, either column or bulging baluster. Roman columns, from 7–8 ft to 3–4 ft or less in length were well known in Roman Britain, and some remain. There is one in the belfry at Wickham; it is about 3 ft 3 in long with rather complex capital and base, with one band near the top. Bulging balusters were also known in Roman Britain. The Saxons must have been familiar with both forms, liked them, adopted them, and in well known characteristic manner, re-expressed the motifs in their own idiom. The result was the double opening with bulging baluster or straight shaft, as characteristic a Saxon creation as can be found anywhere in the plastic arts.

Short bulging balusters were used in Roman Britain for a variety of purposes, as supports for hypocausts, legs of furniture, decoration for tombs, altars, etc. (one is at Housesteads in the Roman wall). An excellent example is on an altar at Birrens (Dumfriesshire) which is bulging, has two half-round bands round the middle and conical-shaped capitals and bases. On the same altar is a horizontal row of astragal ornament looking like a string of tiny balusters separated by two rings between each pair, and what appear to be nicks round the bulging middles. There is a closely similar Roman ornament at Hexham without the nicks, and also a Saxon stone ornament with a series of vertical small balusters, with conical capitals and bases, and between them four rows, at inclined angles, of cigar shaped objects which may be regarded as bulging balusters carried to points at both ends. Similar bulging forms are at York and Jarrow.[1]

Apparently the bulging baluster does not occur at all in the Rhineland area and only very rarely in France. There is one, banded but not apparently bulging, not in a belfry but in the triforium opening at St Pierre, Jumièges,[2] of c 943. Apparently therefore this motif did not come from Europe, though the simple double opening may well have done. Such openings were common in Italy and the Rhineland and France. Good, though late, examples are to be seen in the west front of the eleventh-century (c 1040–66) cathedral at Trier.[3]

Bulging balusters, banded or unbanded, and straight columns may therefore be regarded as specific Saxon features inspired by, or perhaps developed from, Roman forms but re-expressed in their own idiom and used widely for their own specific purposes. The baluster appears to have found more favour in the North. Both kinds were plain or banded, though straight columns rarely had more than one band, if any. The baluster might have two to six, or rarely none. Examples of balusters with none occur at Ovingham, Wearmouth, East Lexham and Worth.

The baluster is so characteristically Saxon and so rarely used except in belfries, that it is apt to be regarded as the most characteristic feature of genuine Saxon belfries, columns only being

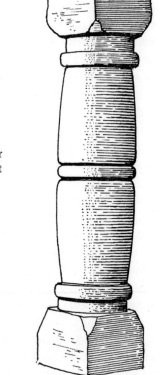

Fig 13. Banded baluster shaft, St John the Baptist church, Greatham

used in the later towers, especially those immediately pre- and post-Conquest. It is true that few balusters occur in such late belfries, but in the earlier belfries, even among the earliest, straight columns are as numerous as, and perhaps indeed outnumber, balusters—even if one excludes Lincolnshire where balusters occur only at Barton-on-Humber. It might be true to say that both forms were used indiscriminately until balusters gradually disappeared under Norman influence which began before the Conquest.

The banded balusters fall into two groups. In by far the majority the bands are raised on the baluster surface, ie, the background has been cut away to leave the bands projecting, so the diameter through the band is greater than that of the shaft. In a few, the bands have resulted from two quirks cut fairly deeply round the shaft, the intervening strip of surface being then rounded off; the diameters through these bands are the same as those of the shafts, ie, the bands do not project. Examples of the latter are at Ovingham where the shaft of the southern opening has an angular flattish band between two quirks near the base; at Oxford (St Michael's) there are central half-round bands between deep depressions on the balusters in both ranges of openings. There are two balusters now used as supports to a modern altar at St John the Baptist church, Greatham (fig 13), about three miles from West Hartlepool. In these the central bands are between two quirks (and so do not project), two others close to the capital and base are of the usual projecting type.[4]

Balusters occur occasionally in openings other than belfries. At Bardsey and Oxford are two ranges, in belfry and ringing chamber. At Barton-on-Humber are three ranges: in ringing chamber, original belfry and in the later Saxon belfry above, which has straight columns. At Brixworth (plate p 107) the opening is triple with two balusters; it is not in a belfry but in the east wall of the third stage overlooking the nave. At Worth there was no tower but the nave fenestration—four windows— was of the belfry type with bulging but unbanded balusters. At Wing there is one in the opening of the nave east gable only slightly bulging and apparently a late form; it has capitals and bases of identical pattern with corners and faces chamfered off to reduce the square to an octagon to fit the circular shaft, with neckings rather than bands, rather similar to those of post-Conquest date at Boothby Pagnal, and more nearly those at Jumièges Abbey. This however does not suggest Norman influence: the cubical capital (not of the cushion type) was rare in Normandy, very rare compared with the voluted capital, while there are many examples of the type in late Saxon England, eg, at Wharram-le-Street (before 1110–1120), Kirk Hammerton (perhaps post-1040), Broughton-by-Briggs (post-1040), Kirkdale (post-1040), St Mary-le-Wigford, Lincoln (pre-Conquest).[5]

Moreover, as indicated above, the double opening with mid-wall straight column, supporting through-stone central impost, was well known in the Rhineland, and to a lesser extent, in France, from where it may have passed to Saxon England. This mode of support is quite different from that adopted in Normandy, viz, of two recessed orders, a method which much later also passed to England but which occurs only rarely in late Saxon belfries (eg, Weaverthorpe and Clapham). As further evidence for the influence of the Rhineland area, Baldwin Brown quotes Trier cathedral where the capital of the shaft is corbelled out, laterally only, to the entire width of the central impost. He emphasised[6] the close resemblance of the capitals at Trier west front and Sompting and considered Trier to have influenced Sompting. The dates however seem to make this unlikely. Baldwin Brown admits there is a question about the actual date of Sompting, and gives the eleventh century; Clapham gives it as probably the first half of the eleventh century. Baldwin Brown dates Trier to the eleventh century; Conant dates the west front to 1039–66. This does not seem to weaken the case for Rhenish influences for this kind of capital (like the Rhenish helm roof) occurs elsewhere in West Germany. This peculiarity is found only at four places in England: Bolam (plate p 54), Jarrow, Scartho and Sompting, where however the corbelled-out capital replaces the impost; the Saxons appear to have realized that not both were needed. Also the Rhenish helm type of roofing a tower occurs at Sompting (plate p 134) alone in England, though there was one at Flixton (Suffolk) and possibly at St Benet's, Cambridge.

According to Baldwin Brown the corbelled-out capital originated in Italy from whence it spread, as so many other features, to west Germany (Trier was at one time a Roman imperial residence and provincial capital city like Cologne and Milan). He mentions its occurence at the ninth-century Sta Pudenziana at Rome and at S Appollinare in Classe, Ravenna. Clapham traces its development back to the early Byzantine feature of the dosseret or pulvino, a kind of plain cubical capital with faces sloping downwards, inserted above the often highly decorated capital of a column to support the arch: ie, like the much later cushion capital, it connected the greater area to be supported above, to the smaller area of the capital or column below, so that the vertical components of the arch stress should be distributed through the pulvino. Later the pulvino was made of one piece with the capital—a feature which appeared later in western Europe as the capital with abacus. It is but a step from the square pulvino to one of marked rectangular form with the long axis running transversely through the wall, like our through-stone impost with mid-wall shaft below, which might or might not have a capital. It is an almost ideal method of dividing a double opening, and seems an obvious development from the impost-capital. It spread to Italy, according to Clapham[7] 'not [perhaps] . . . before the close of the ninth century' where it was used widely in the belfry openings of campanili which began at Ravenna after c 850 and became common in the rest of Italy. It passed to west Germany (where Trier is a late example), and perhaps in the late tenth century, to England.

With the exceptions noted, all the balusters discussed above were used in belfry openings. An earlier type of baluster was developed in Northumbria (certainly there are no remains south of the Tees) in the late seventh century. Their origin is unknown; no comparable features are known among Romano-British monuments. They were circular, of uniform diameter throughout and so well made that some writers consider them to have been turned on a lathe; this is in sharp contrast to the later ones of similar type, especially those at Earls Barton (plate p 90) which are oval, roughly axe-hewn and decorated only on the outer faces. In some the whole of the surface is covered with many bands and hollows. One drawn by Baldwin Brown[8] has twenty-two narrow, and eight wide bands and four hollow depressions. Others have from two to four groups of bands, with two or three bands in each group and with intermediate groups of much finer bands.[9] Only six are known *in situ*, all in jambs at Monkwearmouth: two in the western portal (plate p 54) and four in the east windows in the east face of the third stage. These were the original west windows of the Saxon nave of the tower and appear to have been re-used from elsewhere. About fifty, whole or fragmentary, are to be seen at Wearmouth and Jarrow churches and at Durham Castle museum.

Capitals and bases in belfry openings

Many of the later mid-wall shafts, ie, those moderately pre- or post-Conquest in date, and especially those in Lincolnshire, have capitals and bases which, as in the case with all genuine capitals and bases, are cut from separate stones from the shaft. These capitals are often elaborately decorated with a variety of ornamentation: cushion type or voluted and foliated showing Norman influence, and ornament of more specifically Saxon type.[10]

Of earlier shafts and balusters some have no capitals or bases, as at Bywell-St Andrews and Worth. A few have capitals and bases, crudely cut or built up as at East Lexham; Bolam (plate p 54) has bases of sophisticated bulbous type, three of its four capitals are of the exceptional corbelled out kind (see p 102). Fewer still have capitals only and no bases; one is at Sompting.

A considerable number have bases only, with no capitals. These are usually crudely, even very crudely cut and hardly recognisable as belonging to any particular 'type': examples are at Billingham, Bardsey, Clee, Ovingham, Wearmouth, Appleton-le-Street, Hovingham, Kirk Hammerton, Carlton-in-Lindrick, Oxford (St Michael's), Springthorpe, Caversfield, Bessingham. It is significant that some are cut from the same stone as the shaft, eg, at Wearmouth, Ovingham, Oxford, and are therefore not genuine bases (the 'shaft or column complex' normally consists of three members cut separately—shaft, capital, base).

The scarcity of capitals on the earlier shafts suggests that the early masons were not familiar with this feature. The earliest capitals in this country were probably those on some figured slabs in the Breedon-Castor-Fletton-Peterborough series dated by Clapham to the late eighth or early ninth century, a date now generally accepted. T. D. Kendrick[11] states they were copied from or inspired by the illustrations in the Book of Cerne which he regarded as the first indubitable Mercian MS written and illuminated c 825. Anyone who has seen the book[12] must agree with Kendrick. He would also notice that the artist was familiar with capitals (possibly abroad for there was much interchange of monks between Saxon monasteries at home and abroad) but did not understand their function. His capitals, some almost fantastically elaborate, were purely decorative; one indeed looks rather like a scarf wrapped round the upper part of the shaft. The capitals on these figured slabs were of course not cut from separate stones but formed part of the total carving. Some capitals and bases on mid-wall shafts were very similar to these: they were in fact not functional but purely decorative, an expression of the desire of the masons to give a good and attractive finish to one or both ends of the shaft. This applies also to the much debated baluster shafts at Brixworth and their supposed cushion capitals and bases. These, too, are cut from the same stone as the shaft and are therefore not true capitals. Moreover they do not appear to be even remotely of the cushion type. They were clearly made by axeing the vertical edges of the original block to produce a rough octagon and then cutting the edges of the octagon to approximate roughly to a round diminishing in diameter towards the shaft. The process was like sharpening a lead pencil. A similar procedure was adopted in converting the round base to a square shaft on some of the Mercian standing crosses.[13] The profile is concave (slightly), not convex as a cushion capital should be, and a horizontal cross section through the lower portion appears to be not circular but roughly a square with rounded corners.

The masons of the later belfry openings were clearly familiar with the function of capitals but did not realize that such a function was not necessary in these openings: the downward thrust of an arched lintel is vertical and adequately resisted by the central impost, which in turn was adequately supported by the shaft whether this had a capital or not; a capital was simply not necessary. In the case of voussoired double heads, the lateral thrust would be adequately resisted by the sturdy jambs and adjacent walling.

Openings in ground floors

These are very different from those in belfries. They vary considerably in number and position, but are very similar to one another in type. With few exceptions they are round-headed entrances (or exits), either open arches or rebated for doors.

All towers have openings in the east wall, opening to the nave (or chancel in the case of turriform churches). In a surprisingly large number of western towers this is the only ground floor opening, there being none in the other faces. Among those with no exterior openings are Billingham, Ingram, Ovingham in Northumberland, Morland (Westmorland), Appleton-le-Street, Monk Fryston, Skipwith, Weaverthorpe (Yorks), Glentworth, Marton, Syston, Thurlby (Lincs), Bessingham, Colney, East Lexham, Roughton and many other East Anglian round towers, Carlton-in-Lindrick (Notts), Lavendon (Bucks), Caversfield (Oxon), Bosham, Singleton, Sompting (Sussex). Of these Billingham and Morland have narrow round-headed doorways to the nave; all others are open arches. Why there are no external openings is not known. Obviously these ground floors could not (as so many others do) act as porch entrances to naves; the naves have independent doorways, usually in north and south walls close to the west ends. These ground floors must have been used

Page 107: Above: *(left)* Haddiscoe, belfry opening; *(right)* Brixworth, triple opening in nave W wall from E. Below: *(left)* Colchester, Holy Trinity, tower W doorway; *(right)* Bosham, nave W wall, ie, E face of tower E Wall.

Page 108: (left) Deerhurst, gable-headed double opening in third stage of tower from E; (right) Monkwearmouth, tower lower part from SW.

for special purposes, like porticus. The special use of Barnack (which, however, has an external entrance) is discussed above (see pp 88–9). Other ground floors may have openings in two, three, or all four walls. (Deerhurst is exceptional in having five openings owing to the mid-wall dividing the rectangular tower into two parts).

The remaining towers may be classified as follows:

1 Openings in two walls: east and west, (a) Eastern arches and western doorways. Examples are Corbridge (Northumberland), Kirk Hammerton, Middleton-by-Pickering, Wharram-le-Street (Yorks), Clapham (Beds), Stowe-nine-Churches (Northants), Oxford St Michael's (the former eastern opening here may have been either arch or doorway), Alkborough, Bracebridge, Cabourn, Clee, Glentworth, Lincoln City (St Mary-le-Wigford and St Peter-at-Gowts), Nettleton, Rothwell, Winterton (Lincs), Colchester (both in Roman brick), Earls Barton.
(b) Eastern and western arches, as at Wotton (Surrey) and perhaps South Elmham (Suffolk).
(c) Eastern arch and north doorway, as at Bardsey and Appleton-le-Street (the north opening here may be post-Conquest).
(d) Eastern arch and south doorway: Barnack (Northants), Ledsham (Yorks), Wickham (Berks).
2 Openings in three walls: (e) East and west arches and south doorway: Newton-by-Castle Acre (Norfolk).
(f) East and north arches and west doorway to stair turret: Brigstock (Northants).
(g) East, west and north arches: perhaps Bedford.
3 Openings in four walls: (h) East, west, north and south arches: Jarrow.
(i) East, west, north and south doorways: Brixworth (Northants).
(j) Eastern arch, north, south and west doorways: Caistor (Lincs).
(k) East and west arches and north and south doorways: Netheravon (Wilts).

G

(l) East, north and south doorways and western arch: Monk-wearmouth (plate p 108). Most writers regard these four openings as original and contemporary with the porch. E. C. Gilbert[14] produced evidence in 1964 indicating that the north and south doorway and western arch are later, though still Saxon, than the porch and that the western opening, now an open arch with very early ornamentation, replaced an earlier doorway comparable with the existing east doorway. H. M. Taylor reported, subsequently to 1964, that he had found signs of the original doorway.

Central towers usually have four arches: to nave, chancel and transepts, as at Breamore (Hants), Norton (co Durham), Stow (Lincs), Dover (Kent), Wootton Wawen (Warwicks). In some, two of the arches were reconstructed later in later styles: eg, Norton (east and west arches), Dover and Stow (north and south). Axial towers have east and west arches as at Dunham Magna (Norfolk), Langford (Oxon), Waithe (Lincs). The most highly developed turriform church—Barton-on-Humber (Lincs) —has three doorways, in north, west and south, and one eastern arch.

Circular openings or occuli

Circular openings occur widely in Saxon England in both the towers and naves of many churches. They are definitely a Carolingian feature of nave fenestration. Some occur as additional sound holes in belfries, especially north of the Tees though also in other parts of the country. There may be one, two or three in each face and always above the double openings. At Bywell (plate p 18) and Ovingham there are three in each face; At Cambridge, two (plate p 90); at Dunham Magna and Weybourne, two in each south, east (but not west) wall. At Billingham and Wearmouth, one in each wall. They also occur as windows, not sound holes, in other parts of towers, where they are double splayed and mostly without stone dressings. Good examples are at Bessingham and Roughton (plate p 33). Dover has two ranges, the upper one being in the belfry. Great Hale has a two-splayed one in the north wall, and Burghwallis has one cut straight through the wall (this one may not be contemporary). Hough-on-the-Hill has two double-splayed occuli in the stair-turret.

Occuli also occur in other parts of the church as nave fenestration (in true Carolingian manner) at Avebury (Wilts) and Bosham; single-splayed at Bibury (Glos) and Coltishall (Norfolk). They often occur in nave and chancel gable ends above the chancel arch or east window, as at Bishopstone (Sussex) and Godalming (Surrey). At Stow are large ones in the north and south walls of the north and south transepts. At Barton-on-Humber are two double-splayed ones in the west wall of the western annexe.

The splaying of window openings (fig 6) was functional, not merely decorative. Diffused daylight would enter the outer opening from all directions between nought and ninety degrees to the wall face. Some would be reflected back, ie, outwards from the splay surface, and so lost. The remainder would pass through the central opening and would also be reflected repeatedly to and fro between the inner splay faces and would eventually be reflected inwards into the church interior as a cone of illumination. The angle of this cone would be greater and wider, and the concentration of illumination rather less than if there were no splaying. In dark churches, as Saxon churches always were, a large volume of feeble illumination would be preferable to a small volume of bright light. The Saxon masons undoubtedly realized this and designed their openings accordingly.

Other types of openings

Many other openings characteristic of towers (except in the ground floors) as well as in other parts of the church, are narrow rectangular 'loop' windows sometimes round-headed but more often with flat or arched lintels without stone dressings. In Lincolnshire especially, though also in other areas, the heads are sometimes horse-shoe shaped, ie, key-holed: examples are at Clee,

Glentworth, Marton (Lincs), Langford[15] (Oxon). There are too many such loop windows to list, but a few examples may be given. One of the most striking is Little Bardfield (plate p 135) (Essex) in the fourth and fifth (belfry) stages; these have no dressings, are unsplayed; the crudely built round-heads are of selected flat slabs badly arranged and only just distinguishable from walling. Others are at Bolam, Warden, Wharram-le-Street (which has also a narrow door above the tower arch); and at Cabourn and some other towers in Lincolnshire which are more sophisticated, with arched lintels and proper stone jambs as at Lincoln, St Peter-at-Gowts (plate p 72). In many the jambs narrow upwards, an early feature though curiously, such narrowing is not uncommon in Lincolnshire. Very occasionally such narrowing occurs in window openings as in a window at Brigstock and two doorways at Deerhurst—a large one in the west wall thirty feet above ground level apparently leading nowhere but which presumably formerly opened to an annexe, and another one above the tower arch in the second stage.

Horse-shoe arches

There are references in the literature to horse-shoe arches and window openings in Saxon England. Such a description is misleading and in fact inaccurate. For example, in the tower arch at Bosham (Sussex), the lowest three arch stones on each side are not voussoirs but flat stones running further into the wall than the very even voussoirs above. The sloping of the voussoir joints to a common centre, and the semi-circularity, only begin at the fourth course above the imposts. This has been described as horse-shoed. It is simply a half-round arch on short stilts and should be so described.

The true horse-shoe arch is a more than half-round arch (up to three-quarters-round) which may, or may not, rest on stilts. This beautiful feature, though characteristic of Islamic architecture, was not an Islamic invention but originated aparently in North Syria. According to K. A. C. Cresswell, it was not known in

Sasanian Persia. In 1840, Texier[16] drew and measured an arch of this type (now destroyed) at the church at Dană in northern Syria, dated to 483; here the apse arch was carried round 215 degrees, with a span of thirteen feet. There was one of similar dimensions in the lower façade of Alahan Monastir in Cilicia

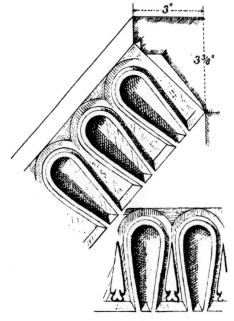

Fig 14. Stow, Jews' harp ornament

(Asia Minor), referred to above (p 19), dated to c 450 or a little later. There appear to be no arches of this type in Saxon England, the nearest approach being perhaps the key-hole openings discussed above. The beautiful so-called Jews' harp ornament (not openings) on the great crossing arch at Stow (Lincs) (fig 14; plate p 71), and also found elsewhere in the county, has some resemblance to genuine horse-shoes, ie, unlike horse-shoe arches, the heads are half-round on tall stilts which narrow markedly downwards. According to Baldwin Brown, the head of the nave south doorway at Limpley Stoke (Wilts) is horse-shoed, he thought deliberately so and 'as assuredly Saxon . . . it must be almost unique.' But the evidence is unconvincing.

Incidentally, slightly pointed arches (ie, two centred, with centres about one-tenth of the span apart), were not uncommon in Islamic architecture. Two may be noted here: at Mshattā, twenty miles south of Amman (Jordan) dated by Cresswell to 743–4, and at Qusayr 'Amra, fifty miles east of Amman, dated to 712–15. These dates give priority of three or four centuries to the East for the invention of the pointed arch; it was not apparently the invention of western 'Gothic' builders.

Unexplained openings in towers

A rectangular doorway, now blocked, is in the north wall of the second stage at Wearmouth. The sill is 11 ft 3 in above ground level and 3 ft below the present floor which was raised at some time. It must have led somewhere.

At Barnack there is a large gable-headed doorway in the west wall rather east of central; it is about 40 ft up and appears to lead nowhere. At Earls Barton in the second stage of the tower are three large tall round-headed doorways. The eastern one, about 25 ft up, may have led to an inter-roof space. Those on the west and south (plate p 90) (there is not one on the north), somewhat lower down, appear to have led nowhere; owing to the elaborate pilaster strip ornamentation on the wall exterior faces, all original, there could have been no attached annexe for the doorways to open to. They remain a mystery. In the stage above the ringing chamber, are four narrower gable-headed openings cut straight through the walls like doorways, but which appear to lead nowhere; they may however be unsplayed windows to light the ringing chamber, which has no other openings.

At St Michael's, Oxford, in the north wall of the third stage is an original round-headed doorway. This could not have led to an inter-roof space being in a north wall. It could have led to a northern adjunct as similarly placed doorways may have done at Deerhurst (west wall), Netheravon and Warblington (north and south walls), though nothing is known of such an adjunct at Oxford or at Deerhurst. There is also one, long since blocked, in the west face of the belfry stage at Bosham. This may possibly have been a single belfry opening contrasting with the double openings in the other faces. The one at Deerhurst apparently leading nowhere is about 30 ft above floor level in the west wall of the third stage; it is now partly above the nave modern ceiling.

6 PILASTER STRIP-WORK

On walls (Lombard bands and blind arcading)

There are eight towers: Barnack, Earls Barton, Stowe-nine-Churches (Northants), Barton-on-Humber (Lincs), St Benet's Cambridge, Langford (Oxon), Sompting (Sussex), St Mary's (Guildford) with walls decorated with flat pilaster strips, of widths varying from 4 in at Earls Barton to over 12 in at Langford and 20 in at Guildford. At Barnack (plate p 89) the strips taper upwards in width from 10 to 11 in at the base, to about 5 in; projections range from 2 in to 6 in. They are nearly all of genuine long and short work; a few are mainly longs.

At Barnack and Earls Barton the strips extend the whole height of the towers, three to six strips on each face at Barnack interrupted only by a single string course; at Earls Barton (plates p 90), three strings divide the strips into four ranges, in each of which the strips are joined above by half-round or gabled heads converting them into arcading. At Barton-on-Humber (plates pp 35 and 36) the strips are on the north and south walls of the lowest two stages only; they have half-round and gabled heads and there is no string. At Langford there is one strip only in the centre of the north and south walls of the lowest two stages. These are peculiar in that they stand on one-stepped bases and meet the strings above with two- or three-stepped imposts. At Sompting (plate p 134) is one in the centre of each north, south and west wall, square cut below the strings and half-round above; there are also two short strips, one on each side of the south-west quoin. At Cambridge (plate p 90) and Stowe-nine-Churches are short strips in the top stages only. Those at Guildford are worth special note. They are of flint, like the walls, 20 in by 6 in on all four walls. They are without doubt genuine buttresses, like the very early ones at St Martin's, Canterbury, though of less projection.

Pilaster strip work also occurs on a number of walls of naves and apses. Among these may be mentioned Kirkdale, Stanton Lacy, Repton, Geddington, Woolbeding, Worth and the apses of Wing, Worth, Brixworth, and Deerhurst; and at six churches in Hampshire: Boarhunt, Breamore, Corhampton, Hambledon, Headbourne Worthy, Hinton Ampnor and Little Samborne[1] The one at Breamore is the only one known to the writer which is of 'upright and flat' work, not 'long and short'. Similar strip-work is found as genuine clasping buttresses to strengthen the corners of the polygonal apses at Brixworth, Wing and Deerhurst.

Baldwin Brown thought that Saxon pilaster work was derived from similar work in Germany known as *lisenen*: the similarity between the work at Earls Barton and that on the western towers at Gernrode is remarkable.[2] But the ornament at Gernrode is modern, though it does not appear to be known whether it was a copy of earlier work or due to the ideas of the restorer. However, Gernrode cannot be accepted as evidence for Baldwin Brown's view. But this decoration occurs elsewhere in the Rhineland, for Clapham pointed out that the First Romanesque style did not spread in France beyond the watershed of the Rhone and Loire; it did penetrate via Switzerland to western and south Germany. So Baldwin Brown may be right, though for the wrong reason. A. W. Clapham accepts Baldwin Brown's derivation and regards it as fully established. Fletcher and Jackson[3] however, regard pilasters as mainly structural, used for strengthening purposes like quoining. They do not accept their direct derivation from German *lisenen* but think that long and short quoining and long and short pilasters are both native products and arose from the same idea of strengthening walls. This seems difficult to accept on the evidence presented.

These writers agree however, that pilasters were used for decorative purposes where strengthening was not required, eg, in the upper parts of towers. Thus it is supposed to be structural in the lower parts of the towers at Barnack and Sompting, but decorative only in the upper parts. (The argument for strengthening at Barnack seems convincing.)[4] It is decorative also at Repton and in the arcading on the apses of Wing, Brixworth and Deerhurst, and in Geddington nave. It is undoubtedly structural at the corners of these apses. There would appear to be only one way to determine in any or all particular cases whether the work is structural or decorative and that is to determine the depth of penetration of the strips into the wall: if the strips are only 'toothed' in they are decorative; if penetration is considerable, say a foot or more, they may be structural. Very little pilaster work seems to have been investigated in this way. Further, why should the Saxons think that their thin walls needed strengthening, just because the quoins required it? The Saxons were magnificent builders, better as such than the Normans a surprising amount of whose work was shoddy. Saxon foundations were strong and their mortar little inferior to Roman. Monkwearmouth tower is an outstanding example of Saxon workmanship. Only 11 ft square with walls 1 ft 9 in thick, not bonded into the nave wall, and 60 ft high, it has continued to stand with no other support than its own good mortar and firm foundations, through nine hundred years of neglect and abuse. How many Norman towers have fallen? To mention just one: at Rottingdean a much sturdier central tower of c 1200 was blown down within a century in spite of being supported by nave, chancel and at least one transept.

Sir Thomas Jackson[5] among other writers, seems to have had a poor opinion of Norman workmanship. He refers to repair work at Winchester Cathedral transept damaged 'when the Norman tower fell as Norman towers often did, soon after it was built,' and to Chichester Cathedral when the spire and tower fell in a gale in 1861: 'the piers were of poor Norman masonry built as usual with bad mortar.' Some Norman piers too, eg, at Winchester, were of a thin shell of ashlar filled not with rubble concrete but with any rubbish available, including even mud. In contrast to this, compare the Norman S–W crossing pier in Peterborough Cathedral, the only foundation of which is the Saxon plaster flooring of the ruined abbey church below. Saxon plaster flooring was indeed good if it could serve as a support, as here, for the enormously greater load of the later Norman church.

The Saxons treated apse angles like quoins and gave them pilaster clasping buttresses; the intermediate arcading was surely merely decorative.

Strip-work around openings

Pilaster strip-work was also used in another way—also quite characteristically Saxon—as 'strip-work round openings' as Baldwin Brown called it. This originated in a single hood-mould, a projecting semi-circular or rectangular moulding above an arch window or doorway, to throw off the rain. Clearly, in view of its function, it was necessary only on exterior openings,[6] but became common later on interior openings such as tower and chancel arches,[7] where it would be decorative only. The hood might rest on the jamb imposts or might end on its own corbels just above the jamb imposts, as at Deerhurst and Bardsey. The Saxons elaborated this feature by continuing the strip-work of the hood-mould below the jamb imposts, down the face of the jambs on both sides, purely as decoration. A good example is at Bywell St Andrew's belfry and the opening in the stage below (plate p 18). Other examples are at Wearmouth, Ovingham, York, Haddiscoe, Billingham, and Wharram-le-Street belfries, and the third stage double openings at Barton-on-Humber. This type of ornament was used widely on tower doorways, as at Middleton-by-Pickering, Ledsham, elaborately decorated with no imposts and passing down outside the jamb imposts; Barnack (plate p 90); Earls Barton (plate p 90), outside the jamb imposts and with multiple hood mould; Barton-on-Humber (plate p 36), north and south doorways; Dunham Magna, gabled; Colchester (plate p 107), turned in Roman bricks; at Kirk Hammerton and Stanton Lacy, on nave exterior doorways. Also on interior tower arches and chancel arches, as at Barnack (plate p 90), Brigstock, Stowe-nine-Churches, Dunham Magna, Dover, Langford (western arch and on one face only), Barton-on-Humber (plate p 36), on inner faces only of both arches, all these are tower arches; at Kirk Hammerton (chancel arch), and Worth (all three arches—chancel and north and south porticus arches). Interior strip-work was often double with one set square-edged and the other half-round; examples are at Skipwith on both faces and at Stow (Lincs) and St Benet's Cambridge on one face only.

'Soffit-roll system' of ornamentation

What may be regarded as a further development of half-round strip-work are half-round rolls or half-columns round arch soffits and jamb reveals, and also round one or both faces of jambs. This may be called the 'soffit-roll system' of ornament. Soffit and associated rolls are normally wider than half-round strip-work which is rarely more than about 5 in across; soffit rolls are 8 in or more. This type of ornament is found in only thirteen or perhaps fifteen, churches: in four or perhaps six tower arches: at Carlton-in-Lindrick, Langford, Netheravon, Sompting and perhaps Repton and Broughton-by-Brigg; in nine chancel arches: at Bosham, Botolphs, Clayton, Selham, Stoughton, Worth (all in Sussex), Wittering (Northants), Syston (Lincs), Deerhurst, and in the eastern arch of the south-central porticus at Deerhurst.

It is not a Norman feature. It occurs at Bernay Abbey (1017–40 or 45) and a few other Norman buildings of the first half of the eleventh century but, according to Baldwin Brown, they disappeared from the Duchy after c 1050 being replaced by the multi-ordered arches with rolls on their edges. The historical development of the feature in England is interesting.

At Botolphs there is a soffit roll only which is attached (not worked on as stated by the Taylors) to the soffit; it does not form an integral part of the head: it consists of twenty-one short half-round stones, compared with fifteen and sixteen voussoirs

respectively on the east and west faces. The joints do not corre-
spond with those between the voussoirs on either face. The
voussoirs are through-stones only as far as the central roll. The
head may therefore be regarded as of three rings (not orders);
an eastern, a western, and a central one which is the soffit roll.

At Selham there is no soffit roll, but three-quarter round
attached rolls run down the jamb reveals. They are not centrally
placed, being 5 in from the west face and 10 in from the east.
There are elaborately ornamented three-member impost-capitals
and Ionic bases. At Sompting (plate p 71) the soffit roll passes
below the jamb imposts down the jamb reveals. The reveal rolls
have capitals of unusual foliate ornament with thin square-cut
abaci above and half-round bases. The soffit roll stands directly
on the abaci.

At Carlton-in-Lindrock and Langford, where the arches are
two-ordered on one face and of one order on the other (or,
perhaps more accurately, the two orders are flush on one face
and recessed on the other), there are in addition to soffit and
reveal rolls, rolls down the recessed faces and round the heads, on
one face only. The Langford rolls have capitals, with thin abaci,
and bases of similar simple but unusual, and perhaps early,
design.

At Wittering, a single-ordered arch, the face rolls are on both
faces with rudimentary capitals and bases. The rolls are not
attached to, but integral with the head and jambs; ie, each
through-stone is cut to full profile and carries the appropriate
parts of all the rolls. Clayton is closely similar to Wittering
except that it is of two orders and the rolls have no capitals or
bases. Here too each through-stone of the inner order and the
corresponding rolls are cut from one stone.

Bosham and Stoughton are two-ordered and the face rolls,
really three-quarter round angle shafts, are in the recesses of
both faces. Here too the rolls are not attached but are cut in one
piece from the same individual stones as the corresponding parts
of jamb and head. The capitals and bases show development from
pure Saxon type at Bosham to Norman (Ionic) bases and capitals

of mixed Saxon and Norman design at Stoughton: the ornament is of trumpet spirals in the round (probably unique in Saxon England) the upper spiral ends being the corner volutes.

At Netheravon both east and west tower arches show this feature though of a very late type. The western arch has two edge rolls (a Norman feature) and recessed angle shafts to the jambs. The eastern arch has two recessed angle shafts and soffit rolls round head and down the jamb reveals.

At Deerhurst there are soffit and jamb rolls on the east door-way of the south-central porticus. This doorway is a later inser-tion of unknown date, perhaps post-Conquest. The blocked chancel arch, which led into the former apse, has jambs with half-round reveals, but no soffit rolls. A similar arrangement is at Worth. Here too the jambs of the chancel arch have half-round reveals—or rather less than half-round. The half-rounds are 2 ft 8 in in east-west diameter, ie, about 4 in (2 in on each face) less than the jamb (chancel wall) thickness, which is 3 ft; there is no soffit roll. These two chancel arches clearly differ in some respects from typical soffit-jamb rolls; it would perhaps be more appro-priate to call them half-round reveals rather than jamb reveal rolls, and to regard them as developments of, rather than included in the soffit-roll system.

At Broughton-by-Brigg the tower eastern arch (originally the chancel arch as it was a turriform church), two-ordered on the west face and single-ordered (not two orders flush with each other) on the east, there are jamb reveal rolls close to the jamb inner faces. These are really independent circular columns stand-ing against the reveals, one face of each square cubic capital being in contact with the jamb face. They have capitals and bases but support nothing; ie, there is no soffit roll or head above, and there is no evidence that such were intended. On the west face there are recessed angle shafts supporting the inner order which has no soffit roll.

At Repton the arrangement is somewhat similar to Broughton. In the south porch are the remains of complete circular columns with square capitals which were built against the jamb reveals of the openings to the original north and south transepts. It is not known if there were soffit rolls. These two churches are rather exceptional. If there were soffit rolls they could be regarded as very advanced forms; in the absence of soffit rolls it is difficult to place them in the system.

German blind arcading

There is another type of early blind arcading quite unrelated to Lombard bands; it is not of Eastern but of German origin. A fine example is at S Simpliciano[8] at Milan of late fourth century date, and two others at Ravenna in the Mausoleum of Galla Placidia[9] of c 425, and in the Orthodox baptistery[10] of c 450. In these the bands and heads are of brick with no imposts or capitals and are flush with the walling; they enclose recesses. Krautheimer describes this feature as 'an articulating device widespread from the third century in the Gallic provinces from Trier to Ravenna.' It is interesting that this type of flat blind arcading spread from the west as far as Ravenna, but no further, where it occurs with the raised type from the East. It did not apparently spread westwards, eg, to Saxon England where the Eastern (raised) form only occurs, at Earls Barton and elsewhere.

Early history of pilaster strip-work

One may look further back than tenth-century German *lisenen* for the original inspiration of pilaster strip-work. *Lisenen* were probably derived from the so-called Lombard band ornamentation of Italy,[11] which was derived ultimately from late Roman work.

Lombard band ornamentation consisted of vertical pilaster strips of slight projection which divided a wall surface into bays. The strips extended nearly the whole height of the wall; at the top, joining the strips of each pair, was a row of two to twelve or more shallow round-headed arches forming a kind of cornice,[12] or sometimes a series of recesses deep enough to cast shadows.

On high walls there might be several ranges of this type at different levels dividing the wall surface into stages. There is a particularly beautiful, though late, example of this on the tower of the church at Pomposa[13] in North Italy, of nine stages dated to c 1063; here the number of arch heads between each two pilasters varies from two to nine.

Blind arcading may be regarded as a variant, or perhaps precursor, of band ornamentation. It was usually around the lower part of a wall and consisted of a series of round- or gable-headed blind arches; each pair of pilasters, or collonettes, would carry a single head, not several as with the band ornament.

A. W. Clapham stated that the earliest example of Lombard band ornament was on the church of San Pietro, Agliate,[14] Italy of c 875. This is a primitive example. A more sophisticated one is at the still earlier church of San Vincento in Prato, Milan[15] later than 814 and perhaps of c 833; here the heads are not round but gabled, as at Earls Barton. This ornament became wide-spread throughout Italy, more especially in the north[16] and spread to other parts of western Europe, with the First Romanesque style of church building; it became perhaps the most striking and characteristic feature of the style. It is found in Spain at Sta Cecilia, Montserrat of 957 or later, Sta Maria, Ripoll[17] of c 1020–32, at Les Escaldus, Andorra, and on the apse of San Pedro del Burgal, Catalonia, ninth to tenth centuries; in southern France at St Michel de Cuixa, St Vorles at Chatillon-sur-Seine, St Hugh's chapel at Berze-la-Ville, at Aime-en-Tarentaise,[18] at St Philibert at Tournus, in the original belfry[19] below the twelfth century top two stages and in the western narthex[20] all c 950–1020; at the tower of St Trophime at Arles[21] mid-twelfth century, and perhaps at St Benigne at Dijon in the eastern rotunda of c 1001–18; in Germany at St Cyrianus, Gernrode, founded 961; the relevant ornament here is around the two western round towers only, which are modern. It also occurs at the Abbey church of Maria Laach founded 1093 but largely rebuilt 1130–56.[22]

Lombard bands did not originate in Italy or with the Lombards. The Lombards did not invade Italy until 568 and Ravenna did not yield until 727. The banding was used in Ravenna before this date, so here it preceded the Lombards.

Banding was known, was indeed common, in Armenia where the arcading was tall, reaching almost to the top of the walling. It occurs in the seventh century cathedral of T'alin;[23] in the sepulchral chapel at Zwart'nots, built between 641 and 666, and in the cathedral at Ani of 989–1001.[24] In Armenia, twin collonettes, not flat pilaster strips, were common and the heads were of rounded profile. All had capitals which were usually double, reminiscent of the Byzantine impost—or pulvino-capital: a relatively large block or cubic capital resting on a smaller cushion or squashed bulbous one—very Saxon-like in appearance. (Ionic capitals were also used, eg, at the sixth-century church at Ptghavank.'

Strzygowski described this Armenian ornamentation as 'an embroidery in delicate low relief after the Persian style [and which] forms a strong contrast with the massiveness of the whole building.' The reference suggests that the Armenians did not originate this particular delicate form of banding; it points its origin to Sasanian Persia AD 224–51, where in fact it was well known.

Blind arcading with blind recesses flanked by engaged twin columns occurs on the façade of the palace at Ctesiphon of the second half of the third century. At Taq-i-Bostan, sixth to seventh century, on a capital, occurs a narrow strip of similar arcading of conch-shaped niches flanked by twin collonettes. It is interesting too that round the face of the huge arch (*iwan*) in the façade at Ctesiphon, is a series of closely adjacent semi-circular depressions which might be described as the round headed type of blind arcading without the supporting columns or collonettes.[25] This spread widely. It occurs in France at Cluny (1088–95), at Montbron (Charente) in the twelfth century, and in England at Castle Acre (Norfolk) also twelfth century.[26] The decoration on the string course at Sompting is closely similar.[27] It was the origin of cusping which became one of the most characteristic ornaments of Cluniac art.[28] The train of travel can

H

be traced: on altars in Hauran of the fifth century, at Corinth, near Rome (found in 1938 beside the path at S Paolo alle Tre Fontane), and on a series of tenth and eleventh-century altar slabs in southern France.[29]

Pilaster-like wall strips projecting from walls were common on western Asiatic buildings from the earliest days of Sumer. The temples at Eridu (level VII)[30] and at Gawrah (level XIII), of early and late Ubaid Period (4000–3500 BC) had walls covered with vertical parallel 'buttresses and recesses' or 'niches and reveals' which became common in Sumerian temples (though not apparently in secular buildings). At the temple of Tel Uquair[31] near Babylon, of early third millennium date, the high platform on which the temple stood, had wide, not deeply projecting pilasters of mud-brick, about 16 ft by 1 ft, wider than those on the super-structure at Eridu or the platform at the White Temple at Uruk of c 3200–3100 BC. Later, after the end of the Third Dynasty at Ur (2112–2021 BC) walls were 'decorated with an elaborate system of attached half-columns divided down the middle by double T-shaped niches carried out in brick, which is an extremely effective form of ornament relying as it does on the varying depth of shadow cast by the sun; it set the pattern for temple builders for centuries to come.'[32] The later junction of the upper part of these strips, each rounded off to join the neighbouring one, gave rise to the blind arcade. This occurs at Feruzabad, early third century AD (built by Ardashir I, the first Sasanian king, before he defeated the Parthians in AD 224 and established the Sasanian dynasty in Persia). Later they were shortened so as not to occupy the whole height of the wall. This was the real origin of the Lombard band arcading. Later still they were superposed, one series on another, as on the façade at Ctesiphon. According to Stryzgowski[33] it became widely distributed from Amman in the Moabite desert (the present capital of Jordan) and north Mesopotamia to Georgia[34] and across the Dobrudja into what is now Czech country.

It is not suggested that there is any kind of 'genetical' descent of band arcading from Sumer to Saxon England. Such a suggestion would not be justified on the evidence available. It is clear however that such arcading was popular and widespread throughout wide areas of space and time. In view of the dominating importance of temple building in these early civilizations, wall decoration must have made a great impression on the minds of the people and may well have sunk deeply to become a folk memory, a memory which could seep upward after centuries or even millennia when an appropriate context arose to draw it to the surface.

To sum up: the artistic influence of Persia on the East Christian area was very great. But Persian motifs when accepted, were re-expressed in the local idioms, whether Armenian or Syrian or Anatolian. Many of these motifs spread westwards via Constantinople to Ravenna and the West. But there can be little doubt that the main disseminators were the Armenians, those great traders, travellers and settlers.

Armenian art and culture and their influences in western Europe

The importance of Armenia to the architectural history of western Europe, including the British Isles, is perhaps not yet fully appreciated. It was Stryzgowski who first opened up Armenia as a country of importance in European architectural history. He, as it were, put it on the architectural-historical map, but like many pioneers of great ability and imagination, he allowed his theories to outrun the evidence then available and his contemporaries were not convinced. In the light of later work (though nothing like enough attention has been paid to Armenian monuments) the climate of opinion has changed towards this country. It is now realised that Armenia, a powerful buffer state between two great empires—the Roman and the Persian—both suffered and benefited from such unpleasant juxtaposition and (like the Jews, a similar buffer state between great empires) developed a culture peculiarly its own. The Armenians owed much to their neighbours Persia, Mesopotamia, Syria and Byzantium but they were not merely borrowers: rather like the later Saxons, they used what they borrowed but re-expressed it in their own national idiom to convert it into a national style or styles of their own. They might be described as good mixers, culturally and commercially, who made their influence felt widely. This is not surprising. There were Armenian colonies in Thrace and Macedonia. Thirteen Byzantine emperors were Armenians or of Armenian descent whose courts contained many Armenian craftsmen and others.[35] Armenians formed the largest and most influential foreign element in the Empire. There was an Armenian quarter or trading centre at Ravenna.

Later, at the end of the tenth to the mid-eleventh centuries, masses of Armenians were transferred by the Byzantine emperors to Cappodocia, and after the crushing defeat of the Byzantines at Manzikert in 1071 by the Seljuk Turks, thousands of Armenians, under their feudal lords, migrated to Cilicia where a kingdom was established which lasted to the late fourteenth century and at one time exercised power and influence as far east as Antioch and Aleppo.

Armenian influence, trade and religious relations increased after the First Crusade and the establishment of the kingdom of Jerusalem in 1100. Many Armenian churches were founded in Florence and even in Rome and elsewhere, and Armenian influence on sculpture was considerable at Cremona and probably Pavia.[36] There was a continuing influx of Armenian refugees into north Italy between 1060 (the date of the occupation of Armenia by the Turks) and 1100 (the foundation of the latin kingdom of Jerusalem).

It is relevant too that Armenia was the earliest Christian state, earlier than Ethiopia. King Tiridates III (Trdat), was converted c 280 by St Gregory 'The Illuminator of the Armenians'; persecutions with the names of Martyrs are referred to even earlier by Armenian writers. Christianity became the official religion in 301 and by 316 Armenia was mainly a Christian country.

Conant describes Armenian architecture as 'the most subtle, finished and impressive of all the proto-Romanesque styles'.[37]

However he does not agree that there was any 'direct influence from Armenia on the Occident'. This, however, would not seem to exclude indirect influence: he agrees that before the Carolingian age 'The Moslem conquests, and later the Iconoclastic movement [717–843] in the Eastern Empire, by expatriating vast numbers of Greeks . . . reinforced the [earlier] eastern element in western art.' Clapham[38] also thought Armenia had little direct influence on Western Romanesque art and that 'it is difficult to trace any element of more distant origin than Constantinople,' a statement perhaps sound enough but which should be considered in the light of the known influence of Armenia on Constantinople (as indicated above); it does not exclude indirect influence. He agrees that 'in the Carolingian Age . . . we have buildings based upon if not imitated from, Eastern models.'

Near Eastern influences indeed, especially from Coptic, Egyptian and Syrian monasteries, and later perhaps from Lérins, are known to have reached the early Irish communities before the coming of St Patrick. Patrick's dates are uncertain but the date of his landing in Ireland is widely accepted as AD 432; Palladius' mission to Ireland was apparently in 431. It seems reasonably clear that there were Christian communities (not monasteries, but collections of hermits in separate hutments forming groups, called 'eremitic monasteries' by Francoise Henry, op cit (c)) in Ireland before and after St Patrick's time and that they reached Ireland from the Mediterranean areas. These early eremitic monasteries were sited in desolate places close to the sea, mainly in two small areas in co Kerry in south-west Munster; in a similar small area in co Mayo in north-west Connacht and the Aran Islands in Galway Bay. The Aranmore monastery was founded by St Enda in the early sixth century and has been stated to be the first Irish monastery in the strict sense[39] (whatever that may mean; possibly as distinct from the eremitic type). A famous one (of unknown date) was Skellig Michael (Sceilg Mhichil) on an island off the coast of Kerry. The cells were of beehive type ie, domed from the ground, built of 'dry' walling by corbelling, similar to the ancient *tholoi* (see p 80). The Mediterranean route at its west end apparently diverged into two branches, one to Galicia in NW Spain and the other to Aquitaine in France; with both these areas the early Irish Church seems to have been in close contact.[40]

The famous 'carpet' pages of the Books of Durrow, Lindisfarne and Kells, (each page covered with a single picture), the wide borders with flat ribbon interlacement, and the numerous red dots used as backgrounds to illuminated initials (used in the West at this time only by the Irish) were due to Coptic influence. Specifically Armenian influences in Ireland are more difficult to detect, possibly because the earliest surviving Armenian illuminated books date from the early ninth century (such books, being portable, were probably a main vehicle for transmission of Eastern influence to the West). Coptic influence however may have been carried to Ireland by Armenian travellers. It is known that many Armenian monks and hermits lived and died in Ireland. The names of many are recorded in Irish Martyrologies.

In England pilaster-strip wall decoration, as discussed above, may have been derived from Armenia via Ravenna and the First Romanesque movement westwards. Armenian influence, though influence from Syria and other parts of the Near East are plainer to see here, may also perhaps have played some part in the decoration of the earliest and most beautiful and sophisticated of the Anglian standing crosses, viz, those at Bewcastle and Ruthwell. These crosses are, and have always been, a puzzle; their ornament was a century or more ahead of anything of the sort in west Europe. Clapham was not prepared to accept this art as 'springing fully armed from the head of a people but recently emerged from a barbaric state,' and 'without any of the preparatory phases leading up to the final achievement.' Where did the inspiration come from? 'Italy and Africa have nothing of the sort to show. Contemporary Coptic sculpture is immeasureably inferior, and Syria owing to its Semitic traditions had little or no figural sculpture of any sort.'[41] This leaves Anatolia and adjacent north-east areas for consideration. Stryzgowski pointed out that Armenia had a fine figural sculpture in the sixth and seventh centuries, which he compared with that of the Northumbrian crosses. Clapham rejected this early dating; in his view there was 'no evidence that Armenia, or indeed any part of Asia, produced such work in the 7th century.' Later authorities however accept this early dating for many Armenian churches and the sculpture, including figural work, which was employed so lavishly as exterior decoration on the churches. There was figural sculpture at the sixth century church at Ptghavank; at the cathedrals of Mren and T'alin of the seventh century, and there are two saints in conversation on a fifth or sixth century stone slab now at Etchmiadzin.

The more sophisticated figure works at Aght'amar are too late (915-21) for our purpose but Nersessian[42] maintains that these sculptures were 'reproducing an early cycle long after it had ceased to be used in other parts of the Christian world.' She points out that one such early cycle is to be found in the paintings of two funerary chapels at El-Bagavat in the great oasis of Khargeh, Egypt, dated to the late fourth or early fifth centuries, and which shows Coptic influence. She concludes from other evidence also that 'early works done in Egypt were known directly or indirectly to the Armenian artists and sculptors.'

The very beautiful vine scroll ornament on the Northumbrian crosses is also of Near Eastern origin. It is closely similar to that on the famous ivory throne of Bishop Maximian, now at Ravenna though probably of Syrian origin (some say Alexandrian, or Constantinopolitan) and of the early sixth century. The ornament reached England towards the end of the seventh century, possibly in the wake of Archbishop Theodore, 669-690.[43]

J. Brøndsted thought the earliest crosses were carved by foreign masons imported from the east Mediterranean area and that later, Saxon masons learnt their job from the foreign masons. Baldwin Brown emphatically disagreed with this; he accepted as all must, the foreign influence, but he was uncertain how that influence was introduced to England and made effective. How the influence was made effective is the real and unsolved problem. All that can be said with certainty is that these great Northern crosses are neither Irish nor Saxon, but Anglian versions of Syrian or Syro-Egyptian or some other, including Armenian, models. As T. D. Kenrick wrote:[44] 'Though the themes used, particularly the vine scroll and the figures, have their origin abroad, it may be truly said that no cross in these islands is without its idiomatic insular stamp.'

Krautheimer too supports the early dating of Armenian churches. He writes: 'The late sixth and seventh centuries are indeed the great centuries of church building in Armenia. Immensely productive in the sheer number of structures, incredibly rich in the variety of central church plans.'[45] He dates Ereruk' to c 550, Ptghavank' to c 600 and Bagaran to 631, and Mren cathedral 639–40. He continues: 'Armenian church building of the seventh century . . . continues traditions established in the inlands of the Near East by at least the fifth or sixth century if not indeed from Roman times.' There were also influences from Cilicia and Cappodocia. In fact 'To some extent . . . Armenian centrally planned churches of the seventh century . . . are embedded in a tradition of church building based on the inlands of the Near East for two or three hundred years.' He concludes: 'On the basis of our present knowledge we should . . . view these centrally planned churches of Armenia as the creation of a local school of architects. . . . All these churches evolve almost simultaneously without manifest ancestry on Armenian soil. Obviously it originated within the complex mesh of political, religious and cultural relationships in which Armenia was involved.' 'Of all the border countries of the Empire, Armenia is the only one to deal with Byzantine architecture on an equal footing. But the differences between Byzantine and Armenian building—in design construction, scale and decoration—cannot be too strongly stressed.'

Page 133: (left) Wickham (Berkshire), tower from SW; (right) Clapham, tower from SE.

Page 134: Sompting: *(right)* tower from N; *(below)* tower from S.

Page 135: *(right)* Bosham, tower from N; *(below)* Little Bardfield, tower from SW.

Page 136: (*above*) Breamore, tower from SW; (*right*) Oxford, St Michael's tower from NW.

Part III   Gazetteer

LOCATION OF SAXON TOWERS

In the geographical lists accompanying the maps, Irish round towers have been omitted, and for reasons apparent on pp 73-4, only twelve East Anglian round towers, representative of about 170 towers in this group, are included.

The architectural list of Saxon towers is hardly more than enumerative, and for further information, reference may be made to the text pages indicated.

Those readers who wish for more detailed discussion may refer to the author's earlier and larger book, *The Greater Anglo-Saxon Churches*, published in 1962 (Faber & Faber), which also includes extensive descriptions of the churches to which these towers are attached.

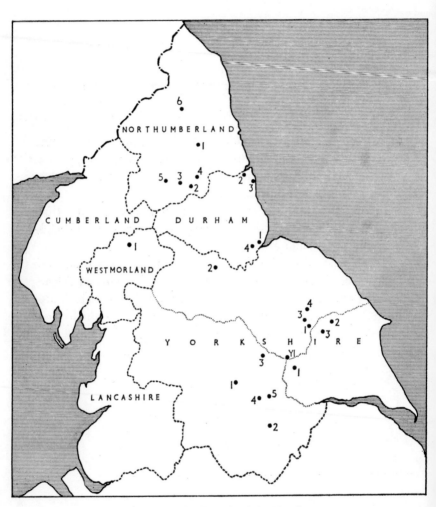

Map 1. England north of the Humber

KEY MAP 1. ENGLAND NORTH OF THE HUMBER

Northumberland
1 Bolam
2 Bywell, St Andrew
3 Corbridge
4 Ovingham
5 Warden
6 Whittingham

Co *Durham*
1 Billingham
2 Jarrow
3 Monkwearmouth
4 Norton

Yorkshire, North Riding
1 Appleton-le-Street
2 Hornby
3 Hovingham
4 Middleton-by-Pickering

Yorkshire, East Riding
1 Skipwith

2 Weaverthorpe
3 Wharram-le-Street

Yorkshire, West Riding
1 Bardsey
2 Burghwallis
3 Kirk Hammerton
4 Ledsham
5 Monk Fryston

York City
1 St Mary the Younger in Bishop Hill Junior

Cumberland
none

Westmorland
1 Morland

Lancashire
none

Map 2. England between the Humber and the Thames:
the Midland counties

KEY MAP 2. ENGLAND BETWEEN THE HUMBER AND THE THAMES: THE MIDLAND COUNTIES

Bedfordshire
1 Bedford: St Peter de Merton
2 Clapham
3 Stevington

Buckinghamshire
1 Lavendon

Cambridgeshire
1 Cambridge: St Benet's

Cheshire
none

Derbyshire
1 Repton

Gloucestershire
1 Deerhurst

Herefordshire
1 Hereford, Bishop's Palace Chapel

Hertfordshire
none

Huntingdonshire
none

Leicestershire
none

Middlesex
none

Northamptonshire
1 Barnack
2 Brigstock
3 Brixworth
4 Earls Barton
5 Peterborough Abbey (Medeshamstede)
6 Stowe-nine-Churches

Nottinghamshire
1 Carlton-in-Lindrick

Oxfordshire
1 Caversfield
2 Langford
3 North Leigh
4 Oxford, St Michael's

Rutland
1 Market Overton

Shropshire
1 Stanton Lacy

Staffordshire
none

Warwickshire
1 Wootton Wawen

Worcestershire
none

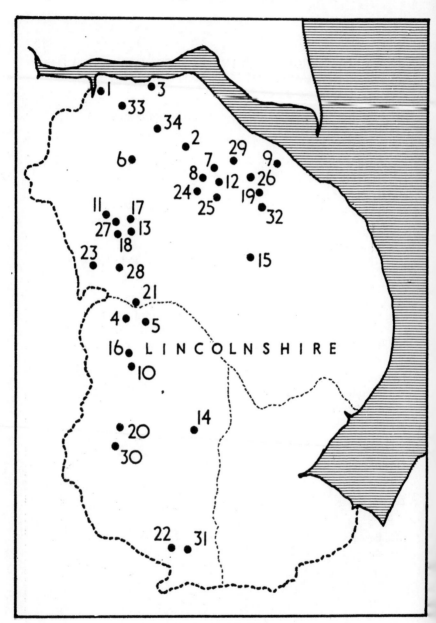

Map 3. Lincolnshire

KEY MAP 3. LINCOLNSHIRE

1 Alkborough
2 Barnetby-le-Wold
3 Barton-on-Humber
4 Bracebridge
5 Branston
6 Broughton-by-Brigg
7 Cabourn
8 Caistor
9 Clee, or Old Clee
10 Coleby
11 Corringham
12 Cuxwold
13 Glentworth
14 Great Hale
15 Hainton
16 Harmston
17 Harpswell
18 Heapham
19 Holton-le-Clay
20 Hough-on-the-Hill
21 Lincoln :
    (a) St Benedict's
    (b) St Mary-le-Wigford
    (c) St Peter-at-Gowts
22 Little Bytham
23 Marton
24 Nettleton
25 Rothwell

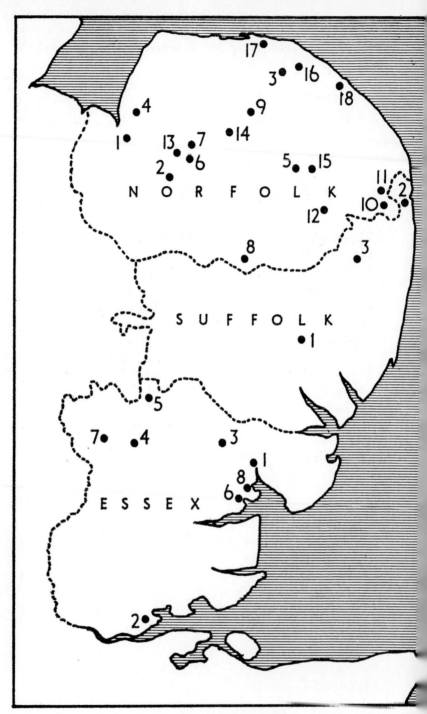

Map 4. East Anglia and Essex

KEY MAP 4.   EAST ANGLIA AND ESSEX

Norfolk
  1 Bawsey
  2 Beechamwell
  3 Bessingham
  4 Castle Rising Chapel
  5 Colney
  6 Dunham Magna
  7 East Lexham
  8 Gissing
  9 Guestwick
 10 Haddiscoe
 11 Haddiscoe Thorpe
 12 Howe
 13 Newton-by-Castle Acre
 14 North Elmham
 15 Norwich : St Mary-at-
       Coslany
 16 Roughton

 17 Weybourne
 18 Witton-by-Walsham

Suffolk
  1 Debenham
  2 Herringfleet
  3 South Elmham, the Old
       Minster

Essex
  1 Colchester, Holy Trinity
  2 Corringham
  3 Great Tey
  4 Little Bardfield
  5 Steeple Bumpstead
  6 Tollesbury
  7 Wendens Ambo
  8 West Mersea

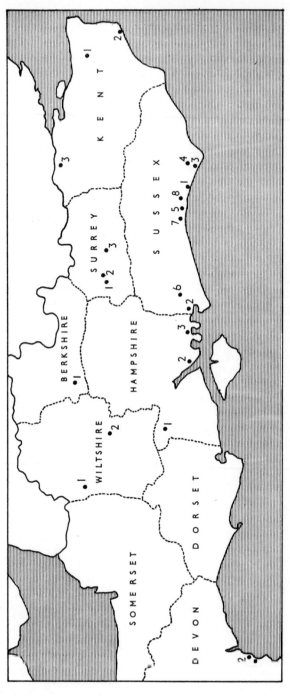

Map 5. England south of the Thames

KEY MAP 5. ENGLAND SOUTH OF THE THAMES

Kent
1 Canterbury, Abbot
 Wulfric's Rotunda
2 Dover, St Mary-in-Castro
3 Swanscombe

Sussex
1 Bishopstone
2 Bosham
3 Eastdean
4 Jevington
5 Old Shoreham
6 Singleton
7 Sompting
8 Southease

Berkshire
1 Wickham

Devonshire
1 Bishopsteignton
2 East Teignmouth

Dorset
 none

Hampshire
1 Breamore
2 Titchfield
3 Warblington

Somerset
 none

Surrey
1 Compton
2 Guildford, St Mary's
3 Wotton

Wiltshire
1 Limpley Stoke
2 Netheravon

SAXON TOWERS AND THEIR MAIN ARCHITECTURAL FEATURES

ALKBOROUGH (Lincs)

Four stages, three string courses. Original belfry in second stage, present belfry in third; top stage later, probably not Saxon, no openings. Quoins, small cubical blocks duplicated here and there. Ground stage very tall, W door with strip work round voussoired head; no openings in N or S wall. Tower arch tall, signs of restoration, voussoired round head with Roman stones in plinth and imposts. Second stage, double openings voussoired round heads, mid-wall shafts with crude capitals on N, S and W; wide rectangular window high up in E wall, flat lintel. Third stage, very tall double openings of thirteenth-century type.

BARDSEY (Yorks, West Riding)

Porch tower, four stages, no string courses. Quoins, massive blocks below, small face-alternate above. No western entrance; original entrance N, unusual position. Eastern arch, single order with hood mould. In east wall, two ranges of belfry single openings with arched lintels; in south wall, two ranges of double openings with voussoired round heads, all with crude bases, no capitals (p 98).

BARNACK (Northants)

Two external stages and two string courses of complex design (plate p 89). Quoins upright and flat. Pilaster strips on all faces, narrowing upwards. No W doorway, main entrance S with round voussoired head and strip work round head and jambs. Interior puzzling (p 88). Tower arch fine, with stripwork round head and jambs, and particularly fine imposts (plate p 89). Gable-headed window in W face. In upper stage: two gable-headed doorways on W and E with no separate jambs; five round-headed openings in S (two), N (two) and W (one). Above these, four gabled belfry openings with no separate jambs but with stone lighting slabs, those in N and S elaborately carved. Square-headed doorway in E overlooking nave.

BARNETBY-LE-WOLD (Lincs)

Almost derelict with more repair work than original. Two stages and one string course. Quoins mainly side-alternate. W door, voussoired head with keystone, unusual in Saxon work. Above is window with arched lintel, and similar ones in second stage N, S and W.

BARTON-ON-HUMBER (Lincs)

Turriform central tower (plates pp 35, 36), four stages, top two separated by string courses. Quoins of long and short work. Pilaster strip work on N and S faces of the two lowest stages, gabled and round-headed. N and S doorways, N gabled, S round-headed, both with strip work all round. E arch to later nave, formerly the chancel arch, pilaster strips all round on W face only; W doorway to annexe with pilasters all round in E face only.

Three ranges of belfry-type openings: in second stage round-headed double openings with double-arched lintels on N and S only with bulging, banded balusters and hood moulds, no side strip work; in third stage, original belfry, gable-headed double openings in all four walls, gabled hoods, no side strips, banded balusters; in top stage, post-Conquest, on N, S and E double openings, voussoired, tall, straight columns instead of balusters, with capitals of curious design. In second stage on E and W large round-headed single openings overlooking former roof spaces.

BEDFORD, St Peter de Merton's Church

Tower now central, originally W with aisle-less nave, now the chancel. A fine example of genuine, long and short quoin in W wall, visible from nave. A little herring-boning in S wall. Elliptically headed wide arch in N wall, of unknown date, perhaps Saxo-Norman. E arch fourteenth century, W modern. Second stage, two blocked round-headed windows in N, S and W walls; and large gable-headed openings in E wall, possibly ingress to former roof space, one jamb stone of which is old standing cross shaft with interlace ornament.

BEECHAMWELL (Norfolk)

Round tower, tall octagonal belfry stage is fourteenth century separated by string from Saxon belfry below; latter with double openings with stone gabled heads, mid-wall thin balusters on N and W, with rough cubical capitals, one shaft is carved shaft of old standing cross; on E and S, heads roughly rounded with flint walling instead of shafts. Very small loop-windows below W and S belfry openings. Tower arch, no distinctive features; above is doorway overlooking nave.

BESSINGHAM (Norfolk)

Round tower, no strings, no external opening in ground stage, on east, tall narrow arch, stone dressings later; above this is gabled opening and a round-headed one in W. Two blocked occuli higher up. Belfry openings, double, gabled-heads with small stone hoods; jambs of small stones with lateral stripwork, no sills, circular mid-wall shafts with no capitals or bases.

BILLINGHAM (Co Durham)

Pieces of carved cross fragments in walls. Four stages, three below the lower (of two) strings. Ground stage, no external entrance, opening to nave, narrow doorway with double-arched lintel. Second stage, narrow W window with arched lintel; formerly an opening in E wall now blocked or hidden. Third stage, large opening with arched lintel in S wall with strip work round head and jambs. Fourth stage is belfry, one large double opening in each wall, arched lintels, strip work round head and jambs as in window below, mid-wall shafts are really long, rect-angular slabs with rounded ends to look like shafts, no capitals.

BISHOPSTONE (Sussex)

This tower was built in first half of twelfth century against an undoubtedly Saxon nave and therefore regarded by most writers as Norman. It is however typologically Saxon and reasons are given in the preface for regarding it simply as twelfth century Saxon. The tower is of tall, slender proportions of four receding stages separated by string courses (Plate p 17). Quoins of slabs of irregular size and disposition; some stones duplicated (a Saxon feature) and in top two stages each angle is cut to form an external angle shaft, ie, a three-quarter round moulding up the external edges, showing perhaps Norman 'feeling'.

No external entrance, a not uncommon Saxon feature. Ground stage windows round-headed modern. In second stage, one in each wall, and third stage in N and S are narrow, loop windows with arched lintels and not very wide single splays; a circular window in W wall of third stage. Fourth stage is belfry, N, S and W openings of usual Saxon double type and instead of shafts are rather wide mullions. The E opening has shaft with cushion capital and base with faces flush with outer wall—the only definitely Norman feature. The E wall below nave roof-level is the original W wall of the earlier Saxon nave, the arch is con-temporary with the tower, is narrow of one order with head of short slabs cut to appropriate shape, ie, not genuine voussoirs, in two rings, E and W, with rubble or flint fillings between the rings—a Saxon feature.

BOLAM (Northumberland)

Quoins, side-alternate slabs. Two string courses but four inter-nal stages, E arch post-Saxon, two modern windows in N and S walls built in blockings of earlier windows. In second stage, arrow-slit windows in N, S, E, W. In third stage, belfry openings double with arched lintels, tall, monolithic, mid-wall, circular shafts with bulbous bases and, except on N, unusual corbelled-out capitals (p 102, plate p 54). In top stage, single light window in each wall with arched lintel on S, gabled on N, E, W.

BOSHAM (Sussex)

Four stages and two strings (plate p 135). Quoins of upright and flat slabs. No doorway in W, N or S; single round-headed windows in N and S. Second stage, windows in N, S and W similar to those below; in the E above tower-arch, a large gable-headed opening with rectangular squint to the S. Third stage, blocked belfry double openings with modern neo-Gothic openings in blocking on N and S, blocked, unexplained opening in W face. Fourth stage, one belfry double opening in W, others are neo-Gothic. Tower arch fine (p 91, plate p 107), stilted round head, upright and flat jambs, no pilaster strip work.

BRACEBRIDGE (Lincs)

Quoins, side-alternate slabs. Short top stage above the only string. Below string, no opening in N or S wall. One window in W wall with arched lintel; below this is W doorway with voussoired head and half-round strip work. Tower arch very fine, voussoired head. Belfry above string with usual double openings, voussoired heads, long mid-wall shafts with elaborate capitals.

BRANSTON (Lincs)

Quoins, face-alternate thin slabs. One very tall external stage and short belfry above the only string. Below string no opening in N or S wall. In W wall, rectangular window high up with flat lintel. W doorway tall and narrow with angle shafts in recesses, voluted capitals, no bases, flat lintel below stilted round head; blind arcading to N and S—all of Romanesque type. In S wall, two large, blocked openings with voussoired heads, perhaps original main entrances. Belfry, double openings in each wall with arched lintels on N and E, voussoired heads on E and S which may be replacements of former arched lintels; circular mid-wall shafts with capitals of cushion type. Tower arch, four-teenth century.

BREAMORE (Hants)

Central tower wider than chancel, same width as nave. Quoins of face-alternate slabs reach to ground, indicative of true central, not axial, tower. Top stage is later timber belfry but may be reproduction of original recessed belfry (p 57, plate p 136). Fine round-headed arch to porticus, head of through-stones but not real voussoirs, cable ornament on impost reveals and Saxon inscription round N face. N porticus arch blocked. E and W arches post-Saxon.

BRIGSTOCK (Northants)

Quoins upright and flat. Circular stair tower on W with two small, rectangular windows on its W. Arches on N and E of tower and gable-headed doorway to W stair tower. Window in S wall of massive jambs and crude voussoirs with (exceptional) keystone (plate p 54). Tower-arch fine, round-headed, voussoired, massive jambs, square cut pilaster strips round head and jambs on E face only.

BRIXWORTH (Northants)

Western porch-tower, originally of two stages, two more added later in Saxon times with a circular W stair-tower of unique design (pp 52–53, plate p 89). Three tiers of small rectangular windows in stair-tower. Walls of mixed rubble and Roman bricks, quoins as walling, some herring-boning. Remains of adjuncts at N and S of ground floor (p 58). Round-headed doorways in N (blocked) S, W and E (tower doorway, not arch), heads crudely turned in Roman bricks. One rectangular window low in S wall and one round-headed, higher up, not one in N wall. Above tower doorway is large blocked opening and above this a triple opening, not a belfry, with round-heads in Roman bricks and two circular baluster shafts with crude capitals and bases incorrectly supposed to be of 'cushion' type (pp 105–6, plate p 107). The present belfry, above the string course, is post-Saxon.

BROUGHTON-BY-BRIGG (Lincs)

Originally turriform with attached W stair-tower. Quoins, large side-alternate slabs. Main doorway in S wall of two orders, round voussoired head, and hood mould, roll mouldings round outer doorway. Two narrow round-headed windows vertically in S wall and one in N wall. Three vertically arranged windows with flat lintels in stair turret. Tower arch two-ordered on W and single order on E. Rolls down jamb reveals on E and angle shafts on W but no soffit rolls; cubic capitals and curious bi-concave bases.

BURGHWALLIS (Yorks, West Riding)

Quoins, side-alternate large slabs. Three recessed stages. First stage, tall, narrow windows with arched lintels in S and W, none in N or E. Second stage, no openings in S or W, one occulus in N. Tower arch not Saxon; above is a round-headed opening. Belfry, curious double openings of later and decadent design: Pointed heads, mid-wall rubble walling instead of shafts.

BYWELL-St ANDREW (Northumberland)

A beautiful tower. Quoins irregular. No W door or N or S. Tower arch not original, reconstructed from old stones. Windows in first stage S wall and second stage W wall with arched lintels. In third stage, S wall is a large opening, arched lintel and round hood supported on vertical pilaster strips. Belfry above the string course in each face has double openings, straight monolithic shafts, arched lintels, hood mould supported on lateral pilasters, circular sound-holes, three in each face.

CAISTOR (Lincs)

Quoins, large, irregular, roughly dressed stones, mixed face and side-alternate. Three stages. Ground stage, very thick walls. W doorway with zig-zag ornament on W face. Blocked voussoired arch head to S of W doorway and similar one in centre of N wall; above this is window with gabled lintel, no other openings in N wall, a similar blocked opening in S wall. Tower arch of one plain order with zig-zag or V-shaped (not chevron) ornament on W face of head as on W doorway. Second stage, a modern window, no others. Third stage, thirteenth century, double opening, small blocked opening above nave roof line.

CAMBRIDGE (St Benet's Church)

Quoins upright and flat. Two short top stages separated by strings. Short pilaster strips on top or belfry stage only. Belfry, double openings in all four walls, single-arched lintels; shallow, bulging, banded balusters which, unusually, are near the interior wall face. Two tall, round-headed windows with shallow, double-arched lintels in each face, one on each side of belfry openings (plate p 90). Fine tower arch to nave; head of voussoirs jambs upright and flat, all through-stones; double pilaster strips round head and jambs, outer ones of square section; inner ones half-round. Elaborate imposts of complex design. Round headed opening in E wall above tower arch.

CANTERBURY

Abbot Wulfric's rotunda. Ruins, foundations only. Octagonal exterior, circular within; an interior ring of eight massive piers and massive half-round towers on N and S.

CARLTON-IN-LINDRICK (Notts)

Fine tower. Quoins, large almost megalithic, side-alternate. Three stages; top stage above upper string is fifteenth-century belfry. Second stage, original belfry, openings double with arched lintels, tall mid-wall columns with simple bases, no capitals. Tower arch fine, round head, soffit roll and rolls down E face but not on W, rolls like angle shafts have capitals with Jews' harp ornament (fig 14). E and W faces of arch really two arches with straight joint between—an unusual feature.

CLAPHAM (Beds)

Tower wider than nave. Quoins of selected rubble slabs laid flat. No strings, four stages (plate p 133). Ground stage, large W doorway with segmental head. No windows. Tower arch plain, one order, voussoired round head. Second stage, single round-headed double splayed windows in N, S and W; a gabled doorway in E wall visible only from interior of this stage— possibly an ingress to third stage from nave. Third stage, a single double-splayed window in each wall. Fourth stage, the belfry, post-Conquest: in each wall is double light, shafts not mid-wall but near outer wall face, the whole under an enclosing arch set back from wall face, cubical capitals with corner volutes; no volutes on N.

CLEE (Lincs)

Quoins irregular, mixed side-and-face-alternate. One string below belfry. Below belfry, one window with arched lintel in S wall, none in N wall. W small round-headed doorway with two rings of voussoirs, an upper and lower, lower one slightly recessed, a hood mould. Above W door a key-hole window, narrowing upwards, single splay, arched lintel. Tower arch, segmental voussoired head in two rings, an upper and lower (as with W door), lower recessed on E face, not on W. Belfry with double openings, arched lintels, mid-wall shafts with cubic capitals and bases.

COLCHESTER (Essex)

Walls of mixed flints and Roman bricks; quoins outlined in thin, Roman bricks. Three external stages, lowest very tall, comprising two internal stages, top two stages shorter and separated by strings. In lowest stage, round-headed windows in N and S walls; W doorway gabled with projecting gabled hood mould carried down below imposts to ground; all in Roman bricks. Tower arch, plain, square-cut round head, with hood mould carried down below imposts on pilasters on both faces, all in Roman bricks. In second, external, stage, round-headed recess in

N and S, two double splayed, round-headed windows in W with a larger similar window between and below, all outlined in Roman bricks. In the taller third stage are two ranges of openings in each wall, the lower, single round-headed, the one in S surrounded by range of blind arcading in Roman bricks. The upper range is of double round-headed belfry openings with rectangular piers of Roman bricks instead of mid-wall shafts.

COLEBY (Lincs)
Quoins tall slabs side-alternate, one string on N wall, two on S. Three stages. Ground stage short; belfry stage tallest. No W door or other external entrance. Tower arch thirteenth century. In S wall above string a key-hole window, arched lintel and chamfered hood with Jews' harp ornament (fig 14). Above is rectangular window above the string. In N wall a tall window with arched lintel, no separate sill. W wall, narrow window only 8 in wide.

COLNEY (Norfolk)
Round tower, flint angle fillings between tower and nave. No strings. Tower arch very tall and narrow, all stone dressings modern; the original Saxon arch was rough and primitive with no dressings. Small rectangular double-splayed windows N, S and W wall but not in E. Belfry openings single, pointed, wide, probably modern.

COMPTON (Surrey)
Very primitive looking. Quoins of thin, selected, uncut slabs laid flat. No string. All windows round-headed, slit openings in the rubble walls, no dressings; one window in each wall high up. Similar windows lower down in S and N walls. Tower arch twelfth century; large window in W wall is modern.

CORBRIDGE (Northumberland)
Porch tower. Two strings only above and below the belfry. Quoins upright and flat. Walls of different lengths. Original W

doorway blocked (modern 3-light window built into it), round-headed with shallow, relieving arch above. Window above with arched lintel, no other opening in porch except the Tower arch which is Roman transferred from elsewhere, head markedly stilted In N wall was a large, rectangular opening now blocked; nothing else is known of this, it may not be Saxon. Between porch and belfry are a small, rectangular window with no dressings in N wall and a similar square one in E wall below nave gable. Belfry openings probably originally double with arched lintels; the present single lights are eighteenth century.

CORRINGHAM (Essex)

A fine, plain, impressive tower, but only very questionably Saxon. Tower arch is small and very plain and might pass equally as late Saxon or early Norman; but the whole is best regarded as early Norman.

CORRINGHAM (Lincs)

Quoins, face-alternate slabs. No original strings. Traces only of W doorway, now blocked. Above is large, rectangular, iron-framed, modern window built into ancient opening. Belfry recessed, double openings, voussoired heads, mid-wall circular shafts with voluted capitals—may be Norman replacements.

CUXWOLD (Lincs)

Much altered. Quoins, side-alternate slabs. No W doorway, the later lancet window may have replaced it. Belfry stage removed at some time. Tower arch plain, one order, may be Norman. No other original openings.

DEBENHAM (Suffolk)

Tall ground stage only is Saxon. Good upright and flat quoins. Tower arch may be original, plain square cut, slightly stilted round-head. Above it, now built up to a narrow slit, was once a doorway of ingress to second stage. No W doorway. Two windows with arched lintels in S wall and one in second stage.

DEERHURST (Glos)

Five internal stages, no string courses. W porch tower, rectangular in E–W direction; two lowest stages separated by N–S mid-wall. Some herring-boning. Three entrance arches W, mid-wall and E; W arch blocked with pointed Gothic arch in blocking, mid-wall arch a modern reconstruction, E arch of square-cut, voussoired head and strip-work hood. Second stage, in E wall above tower arch is doorway with massive single-arched lintel and a small triangular squint to S (plate p 54), remains of gallery on nave wall. Above these, in third stage, is the well known, massive, double-gabled, double opening with gabled projecting hood, massive stepped imposts and massive fluted jambs, no vertical pilasters (plate p 108); this stage possibly inhabited or intended as a private chapel. Opposite these in W wall (of second and third stages) are a small rectangular window, and a large doorway, apparently leading nowhere, with square lintel. Small rectangular windows also in N and S walls of second stage. In fourth stage, no openings in W, S or N but large opening in E wall which led perhaps to roof space. Fifth stage, belfry openings are two-light fourteenth century in blockings of earlier round-headed openings.

DOVER (St Mary in Castro)

Tower quoins of Roman bricks extend only to nave roof level, below which nave and tower walls are continuous, as with axial towers, but tower is central, ie, surmounts a crossing; the lower quoins are of large upright and flat type. Magnificent E and W crossing arches, plain square-cut of Roman bricks with Roman brick pilasters round the heads and down jambs on W faces only. N and S arches are replacements in pointed twelfth century style. Above W arch is large round-headed opening which opened possibly to inter-roof space. Two ranges of window openings; the lower one, Saxon below nave roof apex level, is of circular openings three on N, two on S, two on E, none on W; the upper range in the belfry, of two separate, single, round-headed lights in each wall is, like the rest of this part of the tower, almost entirely of modern rebuilding.

DUNHAM MAGNA (Norfolk)

Axial central tower. Quoins upright and flat, on the W as in all axial towers not continuing below nave roof level. Two tower arches, E and W, as usual in axial towers. Arch heads in Roman bricks, two projecting hoods on W face of E arch, one on W face of W arch. Belfry openings double, mid-wall shafts with cushion capitals and bases of elaborate Saxo-Norman type, partly bulbous. Two circular sound holes above the belfry openings in E and W walls only.

EARLS BARTON (Northants)

Originally turriform. Quoins upright and flat. Of four stages separated by strings, lowest stage of two internal stages. Long and short pilasters, five or six on each face in four ranges separated by the strings and with gabled and round heads resting on the strings (plate p 90); ornamental, not real blind arcading for they support nothing. Elaborate W doorway with massive monolithic jambs with some ornament on reveals, strip work round head and down jambs. E arch reconstructed in post-Saxon times, tower NE and SE quoins to ground indicating former turriform character. In upper part of first stage S wall, is wide double opening with three banded balusters supported on corbels, decorative, supporting nothing (plate p 90). One formerly on W face replaced by the existing Norman one. In second external stage, three large round-headed doorways, one in each E, W and S wall, apparently leading nowhere. In third stage, four gable-headed openings, one in each wall. In fourth stage, the belfry openings are quintuple (plate p 90), one in each face; pieces of walling instead of mid-wall shafts and in front are six banded balusters with no capitals or bases and supported, like those of double openings below, between corbels, purely decorative—they support nothing.

EASTDEAN (East Sussex)

Turriform with apsidal chancel; marks of former apse on tower E wall exterior and on ground below. Fine chancel arch now blocked. Quoins of small roughly dressed stones; three stages separated by strings. Blocked S doorway with flatly segmental arched lintel and jambs of massive blocks two to each jamb, clearly Saxon. Doorway in W and S modern. Windows in W and E of second stage and W, N and E of third stage all similar with arched lintels, one in W very narrow and tapers slightly upwards—an early feature.

EAST LEXHAM (Norfolk)

Round tower roughly built. No external doorway. Three only belfry double openings with roughly made balusters unbanded. with crude capitals and bases.

GISSING (Norfolk)

Round tower of flint. No strings. Three double splayed circular windows in N, W and S walls, no dressings, lower in W is tall round-headed window with stone dressings. Belfry, double openings, round-headed, mid-wall shafts, do not look original. Tower arch tall, narrow, looks Saxon but has later or modern stone dressings.

GLENTWORTH (Lincs)

Quoins of small stones of mixed face- and side-alternate. Two stages, one string. No W doorway (was one originally). Narrow window in W wall with large arched lintel, no sill, massive monolithic S jamb. On E wall interior is tall, narrow, shallow recess, rectangular, simply but irregularly built. In S wall a remarkable narrow key-holed window with deeply stilted double-arched lintel. Belfry openings very tall with voussoired round heads, straight mid-wall columns, irregular jambs and interesting voluted, half-bulbous type of capitals.

GREAT HALE (Lincs)

No original strings, no recessing of belfry. Peculiarly constructed interior staircase. Four small rectangular windows and one circular in N wall, vertically disposed to light staircase. Window in W wall and two in S wall above, similar, with large moulded arched lintels. Belfry openings in all four walls, double, with mid-wall shafts. The capitals are most interesting and varied.

GREAT TEY (Essex)

Lower part only Saxon, of three stages; fourth stage is Norman belfry. Two string courses and quoins of Roman bricks. Was probably originally an axial tower in E position. E and W arches plain square-cut of one order on E face and two, slightly recessed on W. A short portion of square-cut pilaster survives above and below the string on both jambs of E face of E arch. Two round-headed windows in each face of ground stage with, on S face only, a taller, perhaps later, opening between. In next stage in each wall six round-headed, blind recesses, with tiled heads.

GUESTLING (Sussex)

Of doubtful date, early twelfth century seems likeliest; very similar to Bishopstone and of similar date but with rather more Norman 'feeling' (church is contemporary with tower whereas at Bishopstone church is much earlier). Tall, slender proportions with contemporary NW staircase tower. Quoins, small irregular stones, side-alternate with some diagonal tooling. Three stages, one string below belfry. Closely similar windows in N, W and S walls of two lower stages with arched lintels, no imposts, of rather wide internal splay. Belfry openings double of late type, arched lintels, tall, slender not mid-wall shafts (not balusters), cushion capitals and bases flush with wall face.

GUESTWICK (Norfolk)

Now central but originally E axial tower, of uncut flints with quoins of sandstone blocks below and flints at belfry stage,

Marks of original chancel on E face of E wall and on W face of E wall triple strip work all round blocked arch and jambs. W blocked arch plain, partly hidden by later N aisle; above is plain doorway, an ingress to second stage. First and second stages have narrow single-splayed windows in N wall and higher up in E wall, with stone dressings.

GUILDFORD (Surrey)

St Mary's Church. Central tower with wide pilasters of flint on all four walls, are really genuine buttresses. Ground stage, two blocked windows in N and S walls, arched lintels, some Roman bricks in jambs. Two double windows in each N and S wall separated by pilasters. Large belfry openings, post-Saxon, thirteenth or fourteenth century.

HADDISCOE (Norfolk)

Round tower (plate p 53), four stages separated by strings. No external doorway. One window in ground stage, and three on N, W and S of second and third stages, all rather similar with arched lintels. Belfry stage (plate p 107) has gable-headed double opening but dressings are Norman: mid-wall octagonal shafts, cubical scalloped capitals, angle shafts in jambs; double row of Norman billet ornament round each gable-head and down jamb sides. Tower arch (plate p 71) tall, narrow, typically Saxon, plain square-cut, round voussoired head. Above is a large round-headed opening, possibly an ingress to tower.

HADDISCOE THORPE (Norfolk)

Round tower, with segmentally faced flint angle fillings between tower and nave. Three Saxon stages with late Norman recessed belfry above the only string. Ground stage, no indication of W doorway, W window not Saxon. Above are two crudely carved animal heads. Second and third stages, a range of three windows in each stage, tall, narrow, arched lintels, stone jambs, no separate sills. A range of twelve shallow pilasters round the third stage exterior. Belfry, double openings of Norman type, voussoired heads, shafts not mid-wall but near outer face and are banded with central quirks.

HAINTON (Lincs)

Exterior modern repair work. Two recessed stages, one string. Small keyhole window in S wall is only original opening, it has large arched lintel. Belfry openings late Gothic.

HARPSWELL (Lincs)

Low, massive, of attractive plainness; one string. Quoins, face-alternate. Tower arch not Saxon. In S wall above string is tall loop-window with flat lintel, no separate sill. Belfry openings double, arched lintels, mid-wall circular shafts, capitals crudely voluted with foliage and knobs, E opening has flat lintel.

HEAPHAM (Lincs)

Two stages and one string, upper (belfry) stage recessed. W doorway with flat lintel and round head enclosing plain tympanum; the lintel fits between the jambs. Above is keyhole window with arched lintel. Belfry has double openings with shallow arched lintels, mid-wall shafts, badly worn capital with foliated volutes.

HERRINGFLEET (Suffolk)

Round tower. Strings above and below belfry and two courses of rough stone work round tower at nave roof apex level. Ground stage, W opening may be modern; above are two windows N and S, above these three in N, W and S all with rough stone dressings. Small round-headed doorway to nave, plastered. Belfry, four double openings, strip work with Norman billet ornament carried round the heads of each double opening; no strip work on E. Two additional round headed single openings in NW and NE with partial dressings.

HOLTON-LE-CLAY (Lincs)

Much altered in post-Saxon times. Two stages and one string. Quoins, rough and mixed face and-side-alternate. Signs of extensive fire damage. Blocked W doorway now has lancet window in blocking. Above is small opening with arched lintel and a cheap-looking wood framed glass window inserted. Tower arch tall, stilted voussoired head, one order. Belfry stage rebuilt fourteenth century.

HORNBY (Yorks, North Riding)

Late Saxon, four stages separated by strings. Top stage, the present belfry, is fifteenth century. Ground stage, shallow clasping rubble buttresses at NW and SW lower half, thin ashlar slabs above. W doorway with flat lintel and rather distorted relieving arch above. Small round-headed windows in N and S walls, modern. Tower arch tall, massive, voussoired round head. Second stage an original round-headed window. Third stage, original belfry, usual double openings in all four walls, mid-wall shafts with square bases and cushion capitals, arched lintels.

HOUGH-ON-THE-HILL (Lincs)

Quoins, large slabs, mixed face-and-side-alternate. Three Saxon stages with two strings; fourth, the belfry, is later with later openings. No external opening in ground stage. In second stage, narrow rectangular opening with large block lintel. In third stage two narrow tall openings in N and S and two in W walls, with arched lintels. In E wall is large round-headed blocked door-way leading formerly perhaps to roof space. A half-round stair-case tower on W with three vertical tiers of windows with openings of different shapes—rectangular, diagonal, circular— all cut from single stones. No tower arch, only entrance is narrow, thirteenth-century doorway. Within tower is original gable-headed doorway to stair tower.

HOVINGHAM (Yorks, North Riding)

Three slightly recessed stages, two strings. Quoins, large thin slabs, side-alternate. Ground stage: W door two-orders round-headed, plain hood, heavy roll mouldings on W face carried on attached shafts with capitals; inner order plain, square-cut. Very small rectangular window in S wall near string. Above W door and below string is square stone with carved equal-armed (Greek) cross; above this is some herring-boning. Tower arch, tall, narrow, voussoired, plain. Second stage, small rectangular window in S wall as in stage below; in W and S large double-splayed round-headed windows; in E is small opening below apex of nave roof —perhaps an ingress to former roof space. Third stage, belfry, double openings with central shafts of rectangular section, details different in all four walls, no real capitals or bases, heads not arched lintels but primitively constructed arches. In S wall exterior above belfry openings is a carved latin cross which had figures (now badly worn) on the shaft.

HOWE (Norfolk)

Round W tower. Traces of blocked W doorway on both exterior and interior, round-headed, plain square-cut. Tower arch closely similar to W doorway but larger. Above is blocked rectangular doorway, former ingress to upper chamber. Round-headed double splayed windows in N, W and S; circular double-splayed windows in N and S.

INGRAM (Northumberland)

Completely rebuilt from original stones. Two stages, no string. No external entrance. Tower arch wide with two flush arches, the upper one perhaps intended as a relieving arch; narrow windows with arched lintels. In second stage, largely thirteenth century, is a range of small rectangular windows, one in each wall, and above these are thirteenth-century single lancet belfry openings, two side by side in each wall.

JARROW (Co Durham)

W porch tower but now central between post-Saxon nave and original nave of earlier church and now the chancel. Rectangular shape N–S, four stages all Saxon but top stage later than others. On ground stage, plain round-headed arches on N, S, E and W. Second stage, double splayed windows on N and S, the only double splaying in Northumbria, the N one with elaborate Norman dressings added to outer faces; remains of three other openings in E and W. Third stage original belfry (plate p 35) voussoired double openings with shafts, corbelled-out capitals and bulbous bases on N and S, not on E or W: on W is gable-headed doorway, possible former ingress to inter-roof space. Fourth stage, a later belfry has usual double openings, two in each E and W wall, one in each N and S, straight shafts with voluted capitals and bulbous bases, double-arched lintels, the whole set back in voussoired relieving arch above.

JEVINGTON (Sussex)

Some flint herring-boning high up. Two stages, one string. W door modern. Tower arch much modernized, round head recessed on both faces but not really of two orders; strip work round head and down jambs. N and S windows modern but above are remains of two early windows with heads of Roman bricks. Belfry openings modern.

KIRK HAMMERTON (Yorks, West Riding)

Quoins large slabs mainly side-alternate. Two stages, one string. W doorway very narrow, two orders, head parabolic with longer axis vertical, attached columns on face of outer order with geometrically ornamented capitals, no bases; inner order plain. S doorway, voussoired head, strip-work, of long and short work, round head and jambs. Tower arch tall, narrow, plain, one order, parabolic head. At nave roof level are rectangular windows in S, W and N walls; no opening in E wall below belfry. Upper very short stage is belfry, double openings, arched lintels, mid-wall shafts, no capitals, square bases.

LANGFORD (Oxon)

Central axial tower; single wide pilaster strip down centre of two lowest stages of N and S walls, stepped bases and imposts, sundial in S wall. Tower arches in E and W; E one recessed of two orders on W face, single order on E, and with soffit and jamb rolls and with interesting capitals and bases of unusual design; W arch of one order, no soffit or reveal rolls. Third stage, two very narrow double-splayed windows, in each N and S wall, of rubble, ie, no dressings but with central key-holed light apertures of stone. Below in second stage, above the W arch, is large rectangular opening. Fourth stage, is belfry of Norman type, pair of large round-headed openings in each wall with half-round soffit and jamb rolls and on outer faces of jambs and arch heads.

LAVENDON (Bucks)

Very primitive looking. Three stages, no strings. Fourth stage, present belfry, fifteenth century. Some herring-boning in third stage. Quoins of large flat uncut stones laid flat similar to but larger than walling rubble stones. Tower arch, round-headed, plain, one order, square-cut. Above in E wall is tall round-headed doorway opening to nave. Three original windows vertically disposed in each N, S and W wall, one only in the E, all of poor workmanship, heads, jambs and sills of uncut thin stones like the quoins, arranged very badly and irregularly. The top range of these openings were the original belfry openings.

LEDSHAM (Yorks, West Riding)

A porch tower, lowest stage only Saxon. Quoins, large slabs, some massive, mainly side-alternate. No opening in N wall. In S wall is doorway with plain voussoired head and wide strip-work round head and jambs and a continuous band of vine scroll ornament; on interior is a flat lintel. To E of doorway is a window with arched lintel, narrowing slightly upwards; above is a similar window.

LIMPLEY STOKE (Wilts)

W tower, three stages, one string. Top stage with belfry openings probably sixteenth century. The two lower stages show plain indications of extensive repair and restoration work to fabric and openings, which makes deductions of doubtful value.

But the slender proportions (internal measurements: 7 ft by 8 ft), floor one foot above nave floor, thin walls (2 ft 7 in), and massive quoin stones in side-alternate arrangement are all Saxon features.

LINCOLN, St Peter-at-Gowts Church

This church (plate p 72) is so closely similar to its near neighbour St Mary-le-Wigford that a description of Gowts is applicable to Wigford. The two may be regarded as a culmination of the architectural development of that large group of towers known as Lincolnshire bell towers. The tower is tall, slender, beautifully proportioned. Quoins of side-alternate slabs. The belfry is recessed above the only string course. W doorway with round voussoired head, above a flat lintel, is not original, probably replaced an earlier Saxon one as there is no doorway on N or S wall. Tall narrow loop window high up in W wall with arched lintel and hood mould; above is a very worn human figure. A similar window with no hood is in S wall; not one in N wall. Tower arch fine, tall, of one order, voussoired head. Above is large gable-headed doorway, as at Wigford. Belfry openings of usual double type, voussoired round heads, circular straight shafts (octagonal on S); E and N capitals different from S and W, the two latter also different and of curious design. St Benedict's Church nearby was rebuilt on a slightly different site a few yards from the original one, on a smaller scale and certainly not entirely to original design. Present tower squat, of two stages separated by a string. Quoins, variable slabs of mixed face-and-side-alternate. No openings in N or S walls below belfry; crude rectangular windows in W wall of ground and second stages. Belfry, double openings, mid-wall shafts, no capitals or bases.

LITTLE BARDFIELD (Essex)

Squat, Norman-looking tower but Saxon (plate p 135). Five slightly recessed stages separated by strings of rubble. Ground stage, tall with traces of early W door now replaced by larger, modern window. Second stage has no openings. Third stage, two tall round-headed windows in N, S and W walls. Fourth stage, two tall, very narrow windows centrally placed and close together in each wall; fifth stage, similar windows in each wall as in fourth stage but closer together; all with no stone dressings, jambs and sills indistinguishable from walling.

LITTLE BYTHAM (Lincs)

Structurally it is Saxon. Quoins, thin slabs, face-alternate. No opening in N or S below belfry. No W doorway. Two windows in W wall with arched lintels, upper one with hood. Tower arch Norman. Recessed belfry double openings Norman.

MARKET OVERTON (Rutland)

Rebuilt and remodelled in thirteenth and fourteenth centuries on Saxon foundations. Three elaborate, ornamented, Saxon stones built into N, W and S walls. Three loose stones similar to the celebrated Deerhurst decorated opening, lying against tower. Two bulging balusters, probably from former belfry openings, used as gate posts. Tower arch fine, tall narrow with voussoired head and upright and flat jambs.

MARTON (Lincs)

Built almost entirely in herring-boning. Quoins, rough slabs face-alternate in belfry, side-alternate below. One string only below recessed belfry. Below belfry no openings in N or S walls. In W wall high up is original slightly key-holed opening with double-arched lintel and half-round strip-work hood. Above is a stone with human head carved on it. Tower arch voussoired. Above this and below original roof apex is rectangular opening overlooking nave, single slab lintel—lower half visible from nave, upper half only from exterior. Belfry openings, usual double lights with some later features: arched lintel with moulded edges, mid-wall shafts with cubic, not cushion, capitals, half-bulbous below and curious volutes above.

MIDDLETON-BY-PICKERING (Yorks, North Riding)

Three stages. Lower quoins massive, side-alternate. Ground stage W doorway blocked, originally with voussoired head, strip-work round head and jambs; the vesica-shaped window cut into it is post-Saxon. Above is an equal-armed cross on square stone, badly weathered but early ornament is visible. No other opening in W and N below belfry. In S wall two rectangular windows vertically disposed, lower one with no dressings, upper one, flat lintel, stone jambs, no real sill. Tower arch post-Saxon; above is square window also probably post-Saxon. Belfry openings post-Saxon; not known whether these replaced earlier ones.

MONK FRYSTON (Yorks, West Riding)

Four stages, lower three Saxon. First stage very tall. No original openings in W or N wall; in S wide window, pointed outer face and wider round-headed face on interior, outer face probably later insertion. No other opening in S wall. Tower arch c 1400. Second stage, very short belfry with usual double openings, mid-wall columns with cubic capitals, arched lintels— E one visible only from nave. Third stage, very short, no openings—is not a stage but just walling between two corbel tables. Fourth stage c 1400.

MONKWEARMOUTH (Co Durham)

W porch tower of five stages, of three or four Saxon dates (plate p 108). Tall, slender, very thin walls, strings between stages but no recessing of stages. Quoins irregular of big stones side-alternate. Ground stage: four openings, doorways on E, N and S; open, elaborate and primitive looking arch on W which may have replaced earlier doorway (in the Saxon period), W jambs monolithic with primitive carvings and many-banded balusters (plate p 54); barrel vaulted—the only Saxon one above ground. Second stage above carved string course; opening in E wall an ingress from nave, blocked rectangular opening of unknown purpose in N wall, small rectangular window in S wall. Third stage: remains of carving on W wall exterior, no external openings now though formerly one in S wall. Fourth stage, one rectangular opening in W wall cut from one stone, blocked rectangular opening in E wall visible from nave. Fifth stage, belfry, double openings with arched lintels, unbanded central balusters with crude bases, no capitals, pilaster strip work round heads and jambs, one occulus in each wall.

MORLAND (Westmorland)

Three interior stages, two exterior separated by set-back. No strings. Upper half of upper stage is belfry of sixteenth century, lower half the original Saxon belfry with usual double openings in all four walls, mid-wall shafts. No tower arch, instead is tall narrow voussoired doorway of one order. No external entrance. Narrow windows rather low down in N, S and W walls of ground stage.

NETHERAVON (Wilts)

W tower, quoins upright and flat. Two tower arches, E and W, both with soffit and reveal rolls of late, almost Norman, type. Small doorway on N and S which opened to former porticus, remains of which are on the tower walls. Above tower arch is a doorway of ingress to tower or to nave roof space; in N wall is similar doorway, perhaps entrance to upper floor of former N porticus, also a round-headed window in N and S wall. In top stage a small round-headed opening in W face; in the other faces are later double lancets, perhaps replacements.

NETTLETON (Lincs)

Lower part Saxon. One string in E and W, two on N and S. W doorway voussoired head enclosing tympanum with modern filling, strip-work hood with remains of Jews' harp ornament (fig 14) on it. Tower arch, voussoired head with post-Conquest ornament. Above string on W wall is loop window, arched lintel on exterior and flat one on interior. On S wall is another with arched lintel. In E wall is rectangular opening, an ingress to former roof space—one of five only in Lincolnshire.

NORTH ELMHAM (Norfolk)

Ruins only. Former cathedral (fig 9). W axial tower. W doorway blocked, slight remains only of wide E arch and vestiges of base of earlier narrower arch. Half-round stair-turret on S. Remains of two square tower-like adjuncts in angles between transepts and nave, function not known, may have been staircase or flanking towers or porticus.

NORTH LEIGH (Oxon)

Central axial tower. Quoins, side-alternate slabs above aisle roof level, as walling below. Marks on E and W faces of former Saxon chancel and nave. E tower arch blocked of rubble and stones with later post-Saxon pointed arch in the blocking. W arch blocked, few stones only remaining. Narrow windows in N and S walls with double-arched lintels above and in contact with which are relieving arches of flat rubble slabs, flat lintels on interior. High in W wall is outline of blocked opening. Above E arch are remains of an early opening. Belfry openings in all four walls, double-arched lintels with relieving arch above of selected rubble slabs spanning both heads; on interior, jambs and heads are of rubble slabs with no relieving arch; mid-wall shafts with cushion capitals and bases.

NORTON (Co Durham)

Fine central tower. Quoins, fine, massive, well-dressed stones face-alternate. Fine N and S arches to transepts, arch head of long stones cut to appropriate curved shape, not real voussoirs. E and W arches reconstructed in twelfth century. In each wall is large gable-headed opening narrowing slightly upward—early feature unusual in large opening. Above are two openings in each wall, above nave original roof line, with arched lintels to five which have long and short jambs and no separate sills, the other three are rectangular and cut from single stones.

NORWICH (St Mary-at-Coslany)

Round W tower (plate p 72). No original openings below belfry. Belfry double openings of late type, probably Saxo-

Norman: gable heads and jambs of flint rubble, mid-wall shafts with curiously projecting annulus—quite different from the usual Saxon baluster band—round middle, cushion capitals and square bases.

OLD SHOREHAM (Sussex)

At W end was a square chamber narrower than nave and thicker walls, evidently intended to support a tower; probably was a tower. Upper parts and E wall removed by Normans and the space thrown open to nave. Quoins, mainly renewals, irregular side-alternate. No W doorway. Ruins of dressings of blocked Saxon N doorway: round-headed, strip-work round head and door jambs, rough but typical Saxon work.

OVINGHAM (Northumberland)

Quoins, large slabs side-alternate, some stones Roman. Five stages, one string only, below belfry. Ground stage, no external entrance. Tower arch modern. Only Saxon opening is window in S wall with arched lintel. Second stage, window in W wall with arched lintel and monolithic jambs; in E wall is opening overlooking nave. Third stage, no opening. Fourth stage, window in S wall with arched lintel. Fifth stage, the belfry, usual double openings, arched lintels, mid-wall balusters some banded, crude attempts at capitals and bases. Square sectioned strip-work round double openings with monolithic side strips. One circular opening in each tympanum between heads and lights.

OXFORD (St Michael's Church)

Primitive looking but typically Saxon tower (plate p 136). Quoins, SW and SE of selected rubble slabs, NW and NE of large upright and flat slabs. All arch heads and jambs of rough rubble. Blocked W doorway, roughly built windows in N wall of ground and second stages and in W wall of second stage, no openings in S wall of either stage. Third stage, N wall just below the double opening is original doorway apparently leading nowhere. In third and fourth (belfry) stages are two ranges of double openings with mid-wall banded balusters, crude bases, no capitals.

PETERBOROUGH (Northants)

Excavated foundation of Saxon Abbey Church of Medesham-stede beneath floor of Peterborough cathedral, accessible to visitors. Transeptal church but no indications of piers or wall thickening to support central tower. Literary references to tower being consecrated in 1059; this one may have been at the (unexcavated) W end.

REPTON (Derbys)

Quoins of large slab work. Central presbyterial space originally intended to carry a tower, this indicated by opening in E wall above E arch, probably an ingress to inter-roof space. N and S arches led to N and S porticus, attached columns to jamb reveals, lower parts of N ones still *in situ*, upper part with curiously designed impost now in S porch, not known whether there were soffit rolls. Fragmentary but of great historical and architectural interest.

ROTHWELL (Lincs)

Quoins, irregular slabs. Two external stages, one string, tall top stage belfry. Lower stage, W doorway, round head enclosing plain tympanum, strip-work hood. Top half of stage is ringing chamber. Tower arch plain with voussoired head. Above doorway, in the ringing chamber, is small window with high square arched lintel and flat lintel (slab) on interior, similar one in S wall. Belfry, usual double openings, mid-wall shafts with cubic capitals, half-bulbous bases.

ROUGHTON (Norfolk)

Round tower (plate p 53), no string courses, no exterior doorway. Built of flints and pudding-stone. Segmented angle fillings. Tower arch tall and wide, arch head egg-shaped dying into jambs, no imposts. Blocked opening in E wall also egg-shaped. Two occuli double splayed of flints, no stone dressings. Above at height of nave roof apex are three tall narrow, roughly round-headed, windows. Above are double belfry openings gabled with rough slabs. Mid-wall shafts really of rough walling extending throughout wall thickness.

SCARTHO (Lincs)

Quoins, small side-alternate stones. Single string only below slightly recessed belfry. Two stages. Tall lower one has W doorway with round head, half-round strip-work hood. Above is narrow window with arched lintel, also one in S wall. Tower arch fine, double band of voussoirs, an upper and lower, also E and W rings of voussoirs with rubble fillings between. Above is rectangular opening overlooking nave, probably a former ingress to tower. Belfry, double openings, arched lintels, circular mid-wall shafts with no bases but capitals, one on E plain and corbelled-out, others stylised foliate and voluted.

SINGLETON (Sussex)

Quoins, big, stone-work, side-alternate. Three stages, not recessed. Ground stage, no W doorway, voussoired double-splayed windows in N, W and S walls. Second stage, two single-splayed windows in N, not in W or S. In E above the (probably thirteenth century) tower arch is tall gabled opening overlooking nave, probably a former ingress to tower. Belfry, no opening in S or W; in N is single round-headed opening, on E later opening with flat lintel, jambs perhaps original.

SKIPWITH (Yorks, East Riding)

Quoins large, almost megalithic side-alternate (plate p 18). No W doorway, small round-headed window just above and five more higher up—one in W and N and three in S wall with no dressings, except lowest one in S wall which has massive arched lintel. Second internal stage may have been inhabited: large rectangular shallow recess in E wall interior, possibly for altar or ornament, small window near E end of S wall to light recess.

In top Saxon stage is small rectangular opening cut into the blocking of earlier, larger rectangular opening in each wall; this may have been the ringing chamber. The top stage is fifteenth-century belfry which may have replaced earlier Saxon one. Tower arch fine (plate p 36), voussoired round head with double pilaster strip-work round head and jambs, outer strips square cut, inner ones half-round. Large blocked opening in E wall above tower arch.

SOMPTING (Sussex)

Quoins, irregular, mainly genuine, long and short work. SE quoin below nave roof level may not be a quoin but a pilaster as tower is axial. Pilasters are down centre of each face, square-cut below string, half-round above; also two short strips, one on each side of SW quoin. Two external stages, lower one very short below curiously ornamented string course (Plates p 134).

In S wall, one small gabled opening, in N one pair of gabled openings and two single round-headed openings, all below belfry. In belfry in E and W are single gabled openings, two in each face, and on N and S two pairs of double openings in each face with round heads and corbelled-out capitals. Tower arch (plate p 71) of particular interest: rolls to soffit and jamb reveals and curiously ornamented imposts.

SOUTHEASE (Sussex)

Probably of early twelfth century date but typologically Saxon (as Bishopstone). W round tower, one of three in Sussex. No angle pilasters. Lower part of E wall flattened to fit nave. In W is round-headed window of originally narrow splay; above are remains of blocked opening in N wall at nave roof ridge level.

SOUTH ELMHAM (Suffolk)

The Old Minster. Ruin only. Square chamber at W axial to nave probably a former tower (fig 10). Ruin of two windows in N and S walls, single splayed, round heads of flint and rubble, no indication of former stone dressings. Two openings in E wall into nave separated by some feet of walling, no indication of stone dressings.

SPRINGTHORPE (Lincs)

Quoins, small side-alternate slabs. No strings. Original W doorway, blocked, with flat lintel and round head enclosing plain tympanum. Below belfry no opening in W (above doorway) nor in N; in S a window high up in ringing chamber with double arched lintel and plain hood cut from one stone. Belfry double opening shafts not mid-wall, with scalloped cushion capitals and tall cubic bases, all modern reconstructions.

STANTON LACY (Salop)

The present tower and S transept fourteenth century, as is the arch to the Saxon N transept. Not known whether there was a Saxon tower. N transept narrow and is better regarded as a porticus.

STEEPLE BUMPSTEAD (Essex)

An unattractive tower of little interest. Very doubtfully Saxon though some writers have considered it late eleventh century. Four stages, two top ones with much repair work in sixteenth century brick. Belfry openings and tower arch and NE stair turret also sixteenth century. Open and blocked round-headed windows in N, S and W walls of lower two stages, and indications of similar windows in third stage.

STEVINGTON (Beds)

Three stages, only lowest one is Saxon. Quoins, rather rough upright and flat work. No opening in W wall. In S wall is tall, narrow, round-headed, roughly built window; above this is double-splayed window with early, perhaps Saxon, mid-wall wooden light board with round-headed opening, narrowing upwards. Similar window in N wall without a lighting board. Three-light window in W and tower arch are fourteenth century; belfry, fifteenth century.

STOW (Lincs)

Magnificent church, fine crossing (fig 11), nothing known about earlier central tower, if any, above the crossing (present tower later) but so magnificent a crossing was clearly intended to carry a tower. Quoins large, almost megalithic but well dressed, mainly face-alternate. Tall, wide crossing arches, W one (plate p 71) original with round voussoired head, pilaster strips round head and down jamb faces; jamb pilasters—two outer ones square-cut, inner ones half-round; head pilasters, two inner half-round with outer square-cut hood mould with so-called Jews' harp ornament (fig 14) all round it. Jamb reveals of ashlar. Post-Conquest square staircase tower at NE end of nave.

STOWE-NINE-CHURCHES (Northants)

Two stages, one string. Quoins hidden by plaster; a length of carved shaft of old cross is in exterior NW corner quoin. Lower stage tall; in short upper stage are pilaster strips in E and W faces. Blocked narrow W opening with flat lintel in lower stage. Two windows in W wall, upper one round-headed and double-splayed, lower one with flat (renewed) lintel and single splay. Tower arch fine, voussoired, square sectioned hood and vertical pilaster strips down jambs on E face, not on W.

SWALLOW (Lincs)

Quoins irregular but many side-alternate. Two stages, one string. W doorway voussoired with modern tympanum. Above this is narrow window above which is loop window with arched lintel and flat lintel on interior. Tower arch fine, voussoired, slightly segmental, some diagonal tooling suggesting Norman 'feeling'. Belfry stage rebuilt in modern neo-Norman style. No original openings.

SWANSCOMBE (Kent)

Lower part only is Saxon. Flints. Quoins of dressed stone and Roman bricks of rather random arrangement. Very thin walls,

2 ft 1 in thick. No remains of original tower arch. Double-splayed round-headed window in S wall with mainly Roman brick dressings, in head bricks arranged regularly but not pointing radially to a centre.

SYSTON (Lincs)

Three stages, two strings. Quoins much repaired in ashlar. No opening in N wall below belfry. No W doorway. Tower arch fine, apparently Norman. Tall, narrow window with arched lintel in S wall of second stage. Belfry openings double with advanced details, arched lintels and hoods; on S is roll round lower edge of lintel and dentate ornament on lower edge of hood, rectangular slabs instead of mid-wall shafts and angle shafts with simple foliated capitals in jamb recesses. N opening has genuine mid-wall octagonal shafts with voluted capitals, no angle shafts. W opening similar to N. Tower arch fine but apparently Norman.

THURLBY (Lincs)

Large and massive. Quoins irregular but apparently upright and flat. Three stages, two strings; stages of decreasing heights and recessed. No W doorway or other original openings in W, N or S walls below belfry. Window in W wall fourteenth century. Tower arch is now a fine Norman arch built in the blocking of a larger Saxon arch which had voussoired head; some diagonal tooling. Above tower arch in third stage is large, gabled, blocked opening, probably an ingress to inter roof space. One jamb has Viking's head with horned helmet and flowing moustache, probably re-used from elsewhere.

TITCHFIELD (Hants)

Very ancient church with porch. Tower raised in twelfth century; so porch only is Saxon. Quoins, large irregular blocks, some very large, mixed face and side alternate. W doorway, plain voussoired head, no imposts, rough work suggestive of work of early date based perhaps on Roman models.

TOLLESBURY (Essex)

Tower axial. Three stages of which lowest only is Saxon, upper stages late brick replacements. Walls very thick, five feet, and obviously meant to support a tower. Tower arch probably fourteenth century. Relieving arch above is of old materials, maybe from the original Saxon arch, is partly of Roman bricks. W doorway and window above are modern.

WAITHE (Lincs)

Central axial tower. Quoins small face-alternate. Two stages, one string. Low plain E and W arches. Belfry double openings, arched lintels, two to each double opening, openings very tall with thick mid-wall columns with cushion capitals, no bases.

WARBLINGTON (Hants)

Porch tower, four, originally three, stages, very narrow. Ground stage removed, second and third wedged in between later parts of church. Second stage, crudely built round-headed doorways in N and S with dressings of selected slab rubble which must have led to former N and S annexes; W opening, visible only from nave, has thirteenth century stone dressings; above this in wall face, remains of gable-end of former W annexe which preceded present nave, and the W quoins of the present third stage which has thirteenth century lancet windows and so may not be Saxon. Fourth stage modern.

WARDEN (Northumberland)

Quoins, large Roman worked stones. Four stages, no strings. No W doorway, tower arch low round-headed, rough work, slight splay towards nave; imposts of geometrically ornamented Roman bases reversed. Windows in S wall of ground and third stages and in W wall of second stage, none in fourth stage, all with arched lintels on exterior but on interior wide splays, rubble vaulting and angle dressings of Norman type. In E wall of second stage a blocked opening probably former ingress to tower from nave. Fourth stage a belfry rebuilt eighteenth century with single openings in each wall.

WEAVERTHORPE (Yorks, East Riding)

Early twelfth century, ie, of Norman date, beautifully built and with many Saxon features; ashlar built with axed tooling. Three stages, top stage belfry between two strings; lower external stage with two interior stages. Half-round staircase tower on SE corner with three vertically disposed windows on SW. Ground floor, no W door, only external opening is narrow rectangular window with no dressings. Tower arch very tall and narrow, one square-cut order, no imposts, ashlar jambs; above is doorway in second stage with flat lintel, ingress to former inter-roof space. Belfry, Saxon double openings of late design, mid-wall shafts, cushion capitals, voussoired heads, under outer relieving arch.

WENDENS AMBO (Essex)

Of flint with some rubble and Roman bricks. Quoins well dressed stones side-alternate. Three internal stages, two external separated by string. Ground stage, only Saxon opening is fine W doorway, of two square orders, heads of Roman bricks. Tower arch of Norman proportions, construction partly hidden by plaster. Above on W face are indications of original ingress to second stage of tower from nave. Third stage, lancet windows in W, N and S walls built into blockings of earlier Saxon openings which had heads of Roman bricks.

WEST MERSEA (Essex)

Some herring-boning. Quoins have some Roman bricks. Lower part of tower is Saxon, perhaps late. Plain round-headed tower arch of one order, with stepped imposts. A double splayed cir cular window in W wall of second stage, windows in N and S walls. Belfry not Saxon.

WHARRAM-LE-STREET (Yorks, East Riding)

Early twelfth century with Saxon features. Walls rough ashlar squared stones. Quoins similar to walling but of larger stones, side-alternate. Four stages, top belfry recessed above the only string. Ground stage, W doorway very tall, narrow, slightly stilted, narrowing slightly upwards, lower half blocked; head two-orders, inner one square-cut, outer one moulded, above is square hood flush with wall, angle shafts between the two orders with capitals of primitive design, very tall bases of peculiar design.

Tower arch tall, narrow, two orders on E face with angle shafts of peculiar and complex design not unlike those of W doorway; one order on W face. Above in first stage is blocked doorway, stilted head, narrowing upwards, probably former ingress to inter-roof space. Loop windows with arched lintels and moulded jambs are in W and S walls of second stage and in S and W walls of third stage. In N wall no opening below belfry. Belfry openings double, arched lintels, mid-wall shafts, tall cubic capitals, vertical pilasters flanking jambs, not now round lintels but indications that they were originally.

WEYBOURNE (Norfolk)

Ruins only. Quoins of large flattish pebbles or flints with some long pieces of sandstone. Axial tower, E position. In S wall, round head of blocked opening possibly opening to former porticus. In W wall, round head of blocked opening to former nave and above are marks of three former windows vertically disposed; above these, marks of gable of former nave. Belfry openings blocked but dressings visible: double openings, round or roughly gabled heads, no visible mid-wall work, all of flint: lateral arcading to E and W, segmental heads. Circular double-splayed openings, sound holes, two in each wall except W.

WITTON-BY-WALSHAM (Norfolk)

Round W tower, with wide flint angle pilasters between tower and nave. Bonded into Saxon nave and so contemporary, but all the openings are later.

WHITTINGHAM (Northumberland)

Three stages, ground stage only is Saxon. Quoins, irregular side-alternate slabs. No original openings—all destroyed in 1840 rebuilding. Tower arch reconstructed but parts of voussoired head and jambs, of upright and flat work, remain.

WORLABY Lincs)

All rebuilt modern. Tower rebuilt on original Saxon foundations, very fine voussoired head.

WOTTON (Surrey)

Generally considered Norman, but no specific Norman features. Walls of Saxon thickness, lower parts of N and S interior thickened by four inches. Quoins small slabs, mixed side-and-face-alternate. Tower arch roughly built, tall, about 18 ft with tooling by pick, not axe or chisel. W doorway blocked, was similar to tower arch. Narrow, splayed windows, two in N, one in W and two in S, not one in E. Belfry openings not Saxon, probably later, much narrower than tower, of timber with roof, as in tower roof below of Horsham slabs.

YORK (St Mary the Younger in Bishop Hill Junior)

Three stages, one string only below belfry; lower stage with two interior stages. Some herring-boning. Quoins, mixed large and small stones, latter side-alternate. Two rectangular windows in S wall, one in N, in second stage. Tower arch plain, square-cut, two orders, voussoired head, plain projecting hood on both E and W faces, no strip work down jambs. Belfry, double openings, tall, round-headed of slabs not real voussoirs, mid-wall shafts, projecting strip work round heads and down jambs; opening in W wall has upper half renewed as two lancets.

Notes

PREFACE

1 Eg, Prof D. Knowles in *The Tablet*, 22.12.62 and 2.2.63
2 For a discussion of the various types of Saxon churches see E. A. Fisher, pp 29–30
3 Op cit, p 254

PART I

ONE

1 Krautheimer, p 339, n 18
2 For plates see Grabar, p 64, pls 62 and 63; Krautheimer, p 179, fig 70 plan and pls 85 and 88A; J. A. Hamilton p 48 and fig 17
3 L. Bieler, p 9; R. G. Collingwood, op cit, pp 310–12
4 Quoted by Conant, p 301, n 16
5 Op cit, p 295, n 12, pl 1B
6 Clapham *(a)*, p 117
7 C. Ricci quoted by Conant, p 301, n 14
8 Krautheimer, pl 58
9 Simpson, pl 4; J. A. Hamilton, pl XXIX; F. Henry *(d)*, p 55
10 Conant Op cit, p 301, n 15
11 Op cit
12 Op cit *(b)*, p 15
13 C. Ricci, quoted by Conant, p 301, n 14. F. Henry *(d)*, p 55, states that the tower of S Apollinare Nuovo is 'a chronological landmark . . . dated by the monogram of archbishop Giovanni (850–78) carved on the capital of one of the windows.'
14 Op cit *(a)*, p 118
15 References given by Clapham *(a)*, p 116–17
16 E. C. Gilbert *(b)*, pp 9–10
17 Op cit *(a)*, p 87
18 Clapham *(a)*, p 88
19 Krautheimer, p 54; T. G. Jackson *(a)*, I, p 69, fig 16; Simpson, fig p 45

20   Krautheimer, p 62, fig 24; cf also Great Hale (Lincs)
21   Plans in Clapham *(a)*, p 145; Jackson *(a)*, I, p 175; Simpson, p 65; Hamilton, p 41
22   Clapham *(a)*, p 147 and fig 47
23   According to Conant (op cit, p 239) paired towers flanking an apse were a German (Carolingian) invention (but there were two pylons [see below, p 26] flanking the apse at S Vitale). They spread across the Alps to Lombardy where the earliest examples appear to have been at S Abbondio, Como, where however, they were square belfry towers flanking two apses.
24   Plan in Busch *et al*, op cit, p XXVI, fig 11
25   Conant, p 85, fig 27; Clapham *(a)*, p 152, fig 50
26   Conant, p 54 and pl 149 (A)
27   Statham, p 245, fig 236; Busch *et al*, p XVII, fig 3
28   Clapham *(a)*, p 27, fig 9; Krautheimer, p 113, fig 45
29   Stryzgowski, pl 9; Krautheimer, p 229, fig 93A
30   Clapham *(a)*, p 145, fig 45; J. A. Hamilton, pl XXIV
31   Krautheimer, pl 108; Simpson, fig p 30
32   Conant, p 168 and p 173, fig 42, pl 103A; p 295, n 9

PART II

ONE

1   Op cit *(a)*
2   There was a council at Etchmiadzin (then called Vagharshapat) in 451 so there must have been a church there then. There were other churches here: one, St Hrip'simé, was a niche buttressed square with square compartments at the corners (Nersessian *(a)* op cit, p 64, fig 1; Krautheimer, p 231, fig 94A and pl 130). The cathedral was rebuilt in 628 when the wooden dome was replaced by one of stone. Both churches were much altered throughout the centuries.
3   Op cit
4   Krautheimer, pl 17(B)
5   Op cit
6   Almost round *fere rotunda*—in the words of Richard
7   As recorded by Simeon of Durham *(b)* Book II, Ch VI, 'Burnt' does not mean completely destroyed; later, at an unknown date, it was restored by a priest of Hexham. Little is known of its later history (see also Hodges and Gibson, pp 109–14).
8   Clapham (p 148, n 1) wrote that the date 806 incribed in a monument, was proved to be erroneous (in Bull. Arch. 1923) Conant gives 806, based on J. Hubert's paper in *Congres Archeologique* 1930, p 534

9 J. Beckwith, op cit, pp 11–14 and p 221, n 6; he gives references

10 The funerary chapel of S Fructuoso (d 665) near Braga in northern Portugal, was a plain Greek cross, three of whose arms were horse-shoe planned apses; the central tower was domed (Culican, op cit, p 196, fig 13). There was a fifth century baptistery at Tarasa, near Barcelona, of the form of a four-poster raised into a tower surrounded by an aisle within an octagon (ibid, p 189, fig 1). There was apparently a cross-in-square plan at S Miguel, Tarasa, of the ninth century and so too late to have influenced Germigny (Krautheimer, p 245)

11 Clapham (a), p 148, fig 48

12 At St Hrip'simé (618) and S Gayané (c 630) at Vagharshapat (later called Etchmiadzin), and at Bagaran (624–35) (Krautheimer, p 231, fig 94A, B, C; Nersessian (a), p 65, fig 1 (plan), and pl IV 2 (S Hrip'simé); ibid p 67, fig 3 (plan of Bagaran); at Ani cathedral (989–1001), Neressian (a) p 74, fig 7 (plan), and pl II,2

13 J. Beckwith, p 221, n 6

14 Krautheimer, p 245

15 Conant, p 17, p 60; Busch et al pl 67

16 Op cit, p 362

17 William of Malmesbury (Hamilton Ed. Rolls Series, lii, 1870). Gesta Pontificum Anglorum, Liber II; and Leland's Itinerary (1907 Ed.) and Collectanea (Thos Hearn Ed. 1774)

18 Anglo-Saxon Chronicle, Parker Ed. 'A' MS; C (A.B.) Whitelock Ed, 1961; also James Raine: 'Historians of the Church of York' Rolls Series Vol 1, pp 437–8

19 Somerset Record Soc, Vol vii, i, 18

20 William of Malmesbury, and Leland, op cit in n 17 above

21 Krautheimer, op cit, pl 122; Busch and Lohse, op cit, pl 141

22 Op cit (b), Vol I

23 cf E. C. Gilbert, op cit (a)

24 The author is indebted to Mrs Helen Panter of Bath for drawing his attention to Saxon Bath and for supplying most of the information given here. Mrs Panter is continuing her investigations into the identity of the builder of the Abbey Church

25 Chronicon Monasteri de Abingdon, Rolls Series ii, p 272 and 277

26 Clapham (a), p 150, plan, and p 152, plan

27 Op cit (a) and (b)

28 Clapham (a), who gives no evidence

29 E. A. Fisher, pp 254–5

30 Clapham (a) and Gilbert (b)

TWO

1   Op cit *(d)*
2   This dating, based on good historical evidence, is that suggested by
    E. C. Gilbert *(c)* 1947
3   Op cit, 1964
4   E. C. Gilbert, op cit *(e)* 1954
5   Op cit
6   Op cit *(b)*
7   See E. A. Fisher, pp 200–1
8   Where there was a pair of belfries flanking the west door. Accord-
    ing to Conant, 'through Abbot Odo of Cluny and his successors,
    who knew Lombardy well, the square belfry became familiar in N.
    Europe.' (p 55)
9   Op cit
10 The function of these spire-like open-work stages is not clear; did
    they add to the illumination provided by the drum, or were they
    purely decorative as spires are today? At this date they could hardly
    have been bell towers.
11 Clapham *(a)*, pl 31C; Baldwin Brown, p 269, fig 112; p 270, fig 113
12 Clapham translating from a poem by Wolstan, writes: 'a great tower
    in five compartments pierced by open windows, on all four sides as
    many ways are open.'
13 See F. F. Fairweather, op cit
14 Op cit
15 Op cit *(c)*
16 Personal communication to the writer from Dr Cramp. Her findings
    have not yet been published
17 Op cit *(b)*

THREE

1   Op cit
2   Op cit
3   Op cit
4   Op cit
5   Op cit *(b)* pp 28–9
6   de Paor; F. Henry (d); Conant says they were—this is an error
7   L. Bieler, pl p 139
8   Leask, op cit, p 36 and pl I; pp 76–7 and fig 41
9   Leask, pp 148–50 and fig 87
10 Op cit, p 85, fig 44

11 Op cit
12 Op cit, pp 3–4; fig 1
13 Baldwin Smith, fig 63; Statham, pp 71–73 and fig 52. (It was also common in early Christian Ireland, see p 80.)
14 Eg, in some Syrian and Sudan villages, see Baldwin Smith, fig 88 and fig 93
15 Op cit, p 210
16 Horrid phrase. Why not the simpler and more accurate Anglo-Irish?
17 See particularly L. Bieler; Mrs N. Chadwick; Christopher Dawson, ch XI. All op cit
18 Op cit, p 198
19 Op cit *(a)*, p 58. For more extended discussions see ibid *(c)* ch 8
20 See also Eleanor Ducket, op cit
21 See *J Br Arch Ass*, XXXIII, 1927, pl 103, pl II

FOUR

1 Op cit *(c)*
2 See Baldwin Brown, op cit, p 333, fig 149

FIVE

1 Baldwin Brown, p 60, fig 33; p 259, fig 102; p 260, fig 103, 104; p 276, fig 116B; p 261, fig 105. E. A. Fisher, p 279, fig 26
2 Conant, pl 159A. This date has been disputed but is generally accepted
3 Baldwin Brown, p 247, fig 97; Conant, pl 149A
4 I am indebted for this information to Mr Edward Ingram of Sewerby, Bridlington
5 Baldwin Brown, p 409, fig 193; p 397, fig 184; p 408, fig 192; E. A. Fisher, p 128, fig 7; p 267, fig 21; p 285, fig 27
6 Ibid, p 247, fig 97; p 250, fig 98; p 432, fig 202
7 Op cit *(a)*, p 115
8 Op cit, p 125, fig 59
9 Clapham *(a)*, pl 6A; E. A. Fisher, pl 21
10 For examples see E. A. Fisher, op cit, fig 7, 19, 20, 21, 25, 26, 27, 28, 29, 31, 34, 35, 45, and pl 5, 6, 40, 137, 159
11 Op cit *(a)*
12 Now in the University Library, Cambridge
13 See Kendrick, op cit *(b)*, pl XVLI, and especially XLVII, 1
14 Op cit *(a)*

15 E. A. Fisher, pl 112, 113, 143, pp 94–5; and especially E. C. Gilbert (*c*)
16 Quoted by Cresswell, p 75

SIX

1   A. R. & P. M. Green, pl IV, VI, V, III and fig 4
2   Baldwin Brown, op cit, pp 240–43, and fig 95; E. A. Fisher, pp 216–17, and fig 16
3   Op cit
4   E. A. Fisher, p 191
5   Op cit (*c*)
6   As at Cabourn, Clee, Springthorpe, Bracebridge, Lincoln (St Mary-le-Wigford and St Peter-at-Gowts), and at Kirk Hammerton (Yorks), all western doorways; and at Barton-on-Humber, second stage double openings.
7   As at York (St Mary) and Bardsey tower arches, and the blocked chancel arch at Deerhurst
8   Krautheimer, p 58 and pl 12B
9   Conant, pl 27; H. Decker, pl 224; T. G. Jackson (*a*), p 152, pl XXVIII
10 Krautheimer, pp 133, 198; Conant, p 55; Jackson p 150
11 See Clapham (*a*) pp 28–29; Rivoira p 69
12 Conant calls this type of ornament an 'arched corbel table frieze'
13 Conant, pl 137; H. Decker, pl 224
14 Op cit (*a*), pl 7a; (*b*) pl 1b; Conant, p 241, pl 28a
15 Conant, pl 28b
16 H. Decker, pl 1, 7, 8, 10, 11, 12, 15, 18, 43, 81, 94, 183, 195, 217, 224
17 Conant, pl 29B, 32A
18 Clapham (*c*) pl 1a, 2a & b, 3a & b; (b) pl 8b
19 Conant, pl 42; Busch *et al*, pl 201
20 Clapham (*b*) pl 9a
21 Conant pl 88A; pl IIIB
22 Conant, pl 43B, 41A
23 Strzygowski, pl 10
24 Nersessian (*a*), pl V, 2; pl II, 2; (*b*) pl p 66; Strzygowski, pl 16;
25 R. Ghirshman, p 136, fig 172, p 292, fig 375 & 376
26 Joan Evans, pl 47, 48a, 48c
27 E. A. Fisher, p 377
28 Joan Evans, fig 48a shows the relationship
29 Ibid, pp 38 et seq
30 Mallowan (*b*) p 41, fig 30; p 39, fig 28 & 29

31 Andre Parrot, p 97, fig 123
32 Mallowan, pp 12–13, fig 126–8; Parrot, p 201, fig 247–8
33 Op cit, p 62
34 Nersessian *(b)*, p 72, plates of church at Oshki of c 958, and cathedral at Samtavisi of c 1030
35 In AD 989, when the dome of S Sophia was damaged by earthquake, the Armenian Trdat (this name is transliterated in most western languages as Tiridates), the architect of Ani cathedral, was called in to repair it
36 G. H. Crichton, pp 19–20, 43
37 Op cit, p 210
38 Op cit *(b)* pp 107–8
39 D. Attwater, op cit, p 116
40 For further discussion of this admittedly vague period, see Mrs N. K. Chadwick, especially ch 1; Francoise Henry *(c)*, pp 64–5; R. G. Collingwood pp 310-12
41 Clapham *(a)*, p 61
42 Nersessian *(a)*, p 88 and pl 10, 1; p 89, p 95; pp 90–6 and pl XI, XII, 2
43 It should be pointed out that Kitzinger (op cit, pp 61–71 and seven plates) thinks that the motif reached England by a direct route and that the main source of inspiration was a group of late seventh and early eighth century monuments including principally : the mosaics of the Dome of the Rock at Jerusalem (AD 691) and the Great Mosque at Damascus (705), and to a lesser extent the carvings on the facade at Mshatta (now in Berlin) in the Syrian desert (land of Moab) which Cresswell (op cit, I, pp 365 ff and pl 63–78) dated convincingly to the early eighth century.

 Fine scrolls of Syrian type appear early in Armenia, eg, at the mid-seventh century churches of Mastara and Bagaran, with grapes and vineleaves placed alternately in the convolutions of the scrolls (Nersessian *(a)* p 87); this throws doubt on Kitzinger's view
44 Op cit *(a)*, p 127
45 Op cit, pl 230, 232, 235

Bibliography

A list of publications consulted by the author in the preparation of this book. All the items are referred to in the text and notes.

Allcroft, A. Hadrian. 'The Circle and the Cross', ch xxii–iv, pp 189–303, Arch J 2nd Ser xxxi, 1924

Attwater, D. The Penguin Dictionary of Saints. London, 1965

Beckwith, John. Early Medieval Art, Carolingian, Ottonian, Romanesque. London, 1964

Biehler, L. Ireland, Harbinger of the Middle Ages. Oxford, 1963

Brøndsted, J. Early English Ornament. London, 1924

Brown, G. Baldwin. Anglo-Saxon Architecture. London, 1925

Busch, H. Lohse, B. & Wagner, Eva-Maria. Pre-Romanesque Art. London, 1966

Cautley, H. M.
 (a) Norfolk Churches. London, 1949
 (b) Suffolk Churches. London, 1937

Chadwick, Mrs N. The Age of the Saints in the Early Celtic Church. 2nd edn, Oxford, 1963

Clapham, A. W.
 (a) English Romanesque Architecture before the Conquest. 1st edn, Oxford, 1930
 (b) Romanesque Architecture in Western Europe. Oxford, 1936
 (c) 'The Renaissance of Architecture and Stone-Carving in Southern France in the Tenth and Eleventh Centuries', Proc British Academy, XVIII, 1932

Collingwood, R. G. & Myers, J. N. L. Roman Britain and the English Settlements. 2nd edn, Oxford, 1937

Conant, K. J. Carolingian and Romanesque Architecture, 800–1200. London, 1959

Cox, J. C. County Church Series: Norfolk. 2 vols, London, 1911

Cresswell, K. A. C. A Short Account of Early Muslim Architecture. Penguin, 1958

Crichton, G. H. Romanesque Sculpture in Italy. London, 1954

Culicon, W. Spain under the Visigoths and Moors. [In the Dark Ages, Edited by D. Talbot Rice] London, 1965

Dawson, Christopher. The Making of Europe, 400–1000. London, 1939

Decker, H. *Romanesque Art in Italy*. London, 1958

de Paor, M. & L. *Early Christian Ireland*. London, 1958

Ducket, Eleanor. *The Wandering Saints*. 1959

Eddius Stephanus. *Life of Bishop Wilfrid*. text, translation and notes by B. Colgrave. Cambridge, 1927

Evans, Dr Joan. *Cluniac Art of the Romanesque Period*. Cambridge, 1950

Fairweather, F. H. *Aisleless Apsidal Churches of Great Britain*. Colchester, 1933

Fisher, E. A. *The Greater Anglo-Saxon Churches*. Faber & Faber, 1962

Fletcher, E. G. M. & Jackson, E. D. C. 'Long and Short' Quoins and Pilaster Strips in Saxon Churches', *J Br Arch Ass* 3rd Ser, IX 1944, pp 12–29

Ghirshman, R. *Iran, Parthian and Sasanian*. London, 1962

Gilbert, E. C.
   (a) 'Some Problems of Early Northumbrian Architecture', *Arch Aeliana* 4th Ser, XLIII 1964
   (b) 'Brixworth and the English Basilica', *The Art Bulletin*, XLVIII 1965, pp 1–20
   (c) 'Anglian Remains at St Peter's, Monkwearmouth', *Arch Ael* 4th Ser, XXV 1947, pp 147–78
   (d) 'The Anglian Remains at Jarrow Church', *Proc Soc Ant Newcastle-on-Tyne* 5th Ser, I 1955, pp 311–33
   (e) 'Deerhurst Priory Church Revisited', *Bris & Glos Arch Soc*, LXXIII 1954, pp 73–114

Godfrey, W. H. 'Axial Towers in Sussex Churches', *Sussex Arch Coll*, LXXXI 1940, pp 97–120

Green, A. R. & P. M. *Saxon Architecture and Sculpture in Hampshire*. Winchester, 1951

Gunn, R. J. 'Notices of Remains of Ecclesiastical Architecture Supposed to be of the Saxon Period', *Arch J*, vii 1849, pp 359–63

Hamilton, J. A. *Byzantine Architecture and Decoration*. London, 1933

Henry, Francoise.
   (a) *Early Christian Irish Art*, Dublin, 1954
   (b) *High Irish Crosses*. Dublin, 1964
   (c) *Irish Art in the Early Christian Period, to AD 800*. London, 1965
   (d) *Irish Art AD 800–1020*. London, 1967

Hodges, C. C. & Gibson, John. *Hexham and its Abbey*. Hexham and London, 1919

Jackson, Sir T. G.
   (a) *Byzantine and Romanesque Architecture*. 2 vols, Cambridge, 1920
   (b) *Dalmatia, The Quernero, and Istria*. Oxford, 1887
   (c) *Recollections of* . . . Oxford, 1950

Kendrick, T. D.
  (a) Anglo-Saxon Art to AD 900. London, 1938
  (b) Late Saxon and Viking Art. London, 1949
Kitzinger, E. 'Anglo-Saxon Vine Scroll Ornament', Antiquity, X 1936, pp 61–71
Krautheimer, R. Early Christian and Byzantine Architecture. London, 1965
Leask, H. G. Irish Churches and Monastic Buildings. Vol I, Dundalk, 1955
Mallowan, M. E. L.
  (a) Twenty Five Years of Mesopotamian Discovery, 1932–56. London, 1956
  (b) Early Mesopotamia and Iran. London, 1965
Morley, C. 'Circular Towers', Proc Suffolk Inst Arch & Nat Hist, XVIII, part II 1923, pp 144–155
Nersessian, Sirarpie der.
  (a) Armenia and the Byzantine Empire. Cambridge, Mass. USA, 1947
  (b) Between East and West, Armenia and its Divided History. [In the Dark Ages, edited by D. Talbot Rice]. London, 1965
Parrot, André. Ninevah and Babylon. London, 1961
Ricci, Corrado. Romanesque Architecture in Italy. London, 1925
Rice, D. Talbot. English Art, 870–1100. Oxford, 1952
Richard of Hexham: In James Raine: Priory of Hexham. Vol I, Surtees Society, Durham, 1864
Rickman, Thomas.
  (a) 'Further observations on the Ecclesiastical Architecture of France and England', Arch XXVI 1836, pp 26–46
  (b) An attempt to Discriminate the styles of Architecture in England. 5th edn, London, 1846
Rigold, S. E. review of C. J. W. Messant's The Round Towers of English Parish Churches (Norwich, 1958), in Arch J, CXV 1958, pp 264–5
Rivoira, G. T. Lombardic Architecture. 2nd edn, 1933
Simpson, F. M. History of Architectural Development, II: Early Christian, Byzantine and Romanesque. edited by C. Stewart, London, 1954
Smith, Baldwin. The Dome: A Study in the History of Ideas. Princeton, NJ, USA, 1950
Statham, H. H. A Short Critical History of Architecture. 3rd edn, edited by C. M. Aylwin, London, 1927
Strzygowski, J. Origin of Christian Church Art. Oxford, 1923
Taylor, H. M. & J. Anglo-Saxon Architecture. Cambridge, 1964
Thompson, A. Hamilton. 'Brixworth Church', Arch J, ns XVIII, 1912, pp 504–10
Whittingham, A. 'Great Ryburgh Church', Norf Arch XXVI 1938, p XXXIV

Acknowledgments

Acknowledgments and thanks are due to the following for supplying photographs and/or for permission to publish copyright material:

Bord Failte Eireann (p 17 left); National Buildings Record, and Royal Commission on Historical Monuments by permission of the Controller of HMSO (pp 17 right, 35 right, 36 bottom right, 53 right, 71 bottom right, 72 left, 90 bottom left, 107 top left, bottom right, 133 left, 135 bottom, 136 top, bottom); Mrs F. H. Crossley (p 18 top); C. E. Coulthard (pp 18 bottom, 35 left, 36 top left, bottom left, 54 bottom right, 71 top left, top right, bottom left, 72 right, 89 left, 90 bottom right, 107 top right, bottom left, 108 right, 134 top); Hants Field Club and Archaeological Soc (p 36 top right); E. C. Le Grice (p 53 left); Bruce Allsopp, B Arch, FRIBA (p 54 top left, bottom left); Mrs D. D. Hinton (p 54 top right); W. A. Call (pp 89 right, 90 top left, top right); Courtauld Institute of Art (p 108 left); J. E. Edmunds (p 133 right); R. de Z. Hall (p 134 bottom); F. Goldring (p 135 top).

Special thanks are due to Mr Coulthard. The fifteen plates reproduced are from more than a hundred generously placed at the author's disposal from Mr Coulthard's vast collection of photographs of Saxon churches and details.

Figure 5 (types of quoining) is after E. C. Gilbert, *Arch Ael*, 1946; figures 1, 2, 3, 4 and 8 are from *English Romanesque Architecture before the Conquest* by A. W. Clapham, by permission of the Clarendon Press, Oxford; figure 9 is reproduced by permission of (the late) W. H. Godfrey, CBE; figure 10 is after C. R. Peers, *Arch J*, 1901; figure 12 is by permission of the Rev D. E. Hood; figure 14 is from G. Atkinson, *Antiquaries' Journal*, vi, 1850.

Mrs Helen Panter supplied the information about Saxon Bath Abbey and Limpley Stoke tower.

Index of Persons

Plate references are printed in italic

Acca, prior of Hexham, 30
Aidan, 29
Alcuin, of York, 31, 32
Aldhune, bp of Chester-le-Street, 51
Aldwine, abbot of Jarrow, 50, 67
Alfred, k, 37, 38
Ambrose, St, bp of Milan, 19
Arachis II, k of Lombardy, 33
Ardashir I, k of Persia, 126
Atreus, of Mycenae, 80
Attila, k of Huns, 19

Bede, the Venerable, 29, 30
Benedict Biscop, 30
Boniface, St [Wynfrith], 26

Canute, k of England, 43
Charlemagne, emperor, 23, 25, 31, 38, 93
Constantina, d of Constantine the Great, 19
Constantine, the Great, 16, 19

Dunstan, St, 24

Eadwig, k of England, 34
Earl Roger, 12
Eddius Stephanus, 30, 63
Edgar, k of England, 34
Edmund, St, k of East Anglia, 38
Edward, the Confessor, 11
Edwin, k of Northumbria, 29
Enda, St, abbot of Avanmore, 129
Ethelwold, abbot of Abingdon, 38
Ethelwold, bp of Winchester, 24, 57

Galerius, emperor, 25
Giovanni, archbishop, 185 n 13
Gregory, St, the Illuminator, 128

Heane, thegn, 38
Heathered, bp of Worcester, 34
Honoratus, St, 20

Justin II, emperor, 31

Maximian, bp, 131

Odo, abbot of Cluny, 23, 188 n 8; archbishop Canterbury, 24, 56
Offa, k of Mercia, 34, 93

Palladius, 129
Patrick, St, 20, 129
Paulinus, 29, 30

Richard, prior of Hexham, 30, 63
Robert of Lorraine, bp of Hereford, 38

Scotland, abbot of Canterbury, 39
Simeon of Durham, 186 n 7
Suger, abbot of St Denis, 20, 22

Theodore, archbishop of Canterbury, 13, 30, 38, 131
Theoduld, founder of Germigny-des-Prés, 31, 33
Trdat [Tiridates], Armenian architect, 191 n 35
Trdat III [Tiridates], k of Armenia, 128

Wilfrid, of Ripon, 30, 37, 55, 63
William, the Conqueror, 50
Wulfred, abbot of Canterbury, 24
Wulfric, abbot of Canterbury, 39
Wynfrith, *see* Boniface

Index of Places and Sites

Aachen, palace chapel, 23, 25, 31, 32, 33, 37, 63, 68, 93
Abbeville, *see* St Riquier
Abernethy, round tower, 79
Abingdon, abbey, 38
Aghowle, 79
Aght'amar, cathedral, 131
Agliate, San Pietro, 124
Aime-en-Tarentaise, 124
Alahan Monastir, 19, 113
Aleppo, 128
Alkborough, 95, 97, 109, 143, 148
Amman [Jordan], 126
Andorra, 26, 75, 124
Ani, cathedral, 125, 187 n 12, 191 n 35
Annegray, abbey, 79
Antioch, 16, 128
Appleton-le-Street, 96, 104, 106, 109, 139
Aquitaine, 130
Aranmore, monastery, 129
Ardmore, round tower, 77
Arles, 19; St Trophime, 124
Armenia, *see* General and Architectural Index
Arpachiyah, 80
Athelney, Alfred's church, 37, 38
Avebury, 111

Bagaran, ch with vine scroll, 132, 187 n 12, 191 n 43
Bardsey, 49, 51, 97, 98, 101, 104, 109, 119, 139, 148, 190 n 7.
Barnack, 42, 43, 45, 57, 87, 88, 94, 109, 114, 116, 118, 119, 120, 141, 148, 89, 90
Barnetby-le-Wold, 143, 149
Barton-on-Humber, turriform ch, 43, 44, 57, 69, 94, 95, 96, 97, 100, 101, 110, 111, 116, 119, 120, 143, 149, 190 n 6, 35, 36

Bath, abbey, 34, 187
Bawsey, 145
Bedford, 94, 109, 141, 149
Beechamwell, 145, 150
Benevento [Italy], 33
Bernay, abbey, 120
Berze-la-Ville, St Hugh's chapel, 124
Bessingham, round tower, 73, 76, 94, 97, 104, 106, 110, 119, 120, 150
Bewcastle, cross, 130
Bibury, 111
Billingham, 85, 94, 96, 104, 106, 110, 119, 139, 150
Birrens, 99
Bishopsteignton, 84, 147
Bishopstone, ch 10, 66, 111, 147, 151, 17
Boarhunt, 62, 117
Bobbio, monastery, 79
Bolam, 96, 102, 104, 112, 139, 151, 54
Boothby Pagnal, 101
Bosham, 12, 91, 94, 95, 97, 106, 111, 112, 115, 120, 121, 147, 152, 106, 135
Botolphs, soffit rolls, 120
Bracebridge, 97, 109, 143, 152, 190 n 6.
Braga [Portugal] S Fructuoso, 187 n 10
Branston, 87, 97, 143, 152
Breamore, 47, 57, 60, 62, 110, 117, 147, 153, 71, 136
Brechin, round tower, 79
Bredon, 105
Brigstock, 41, 63, 65, 94, 109, 112, 120, 141, 153, 54
Brixworth, 47, 49, 52, 55, 56, 64, 65, 68, 92, 93, 94, 101, 105, 109, 117, 118, 141, 153, 89, 107

Broughton-by-Brigg, turriform ch, 45, 64, 65, 102, 120, 122, 143, 154

Burghwallis, 94, 97, 111, 139, 154

Burgundy, *see* Cluny

Bury St Edmunds, tomb chapel, 38

Bywell, St Andrews, 85, 94, 96, 104, 110, 119, 139, 154, 18; St Peters, 67

Cabourn, 109, 112, 143, 190 n 6

Caistor, 58, 59, 88, 109, 143, 154

Cambridge, St Benet's, 42, 58, 94, 96, 102, 110, 116, 120, 141, 155, 90

Cannes, 20

Canterbury, Abbot Wulfric's rotunda, 39, 147, 155; cathedral, lateral towers, 24, 56, 88; St Martin's ch, 117; St Mildred's ch, 39, 36

Carlton-in-Lindrick, 85, 96, 104, 106, 120, 121, 141, 155

Castle Acre, 74, 125

Castledermot, round towers, 77

Castle Rising, chapel, 60, 61, 145

Catalonia, San Pietro del Burgal, 75, 124

Caversfield, 85, 104, 106, 141

Centula, *see* St Riquier

Chatillon-sur-Seine, St Vorles, 124

Chester-le-Street, 51

Chichester, cath, 93, 118; seal, 57

Cilicia, kingdom of, 19

Clapham, 58, 59, 94, 97, 102, 109, 141, 156, 133

Clayton, 12, 120, 121

Clee, Old, 59, 96, 104, 109, 111, 143, 156, 190 n 6

Climping, 12

Clonmacnoise, round tower, at St Finghan's ch, 78

Cluny, abbey, 23, 24, 55, 125, 188 n 8

Colchester, 97, 109, 119, 145, 156, 107

Coleby, 157

Colney, 73, 74, 76, 106, 145, 157

Cologne, 103; St Gerean ch, 25

Coltishall, 111

Como, St Abbondio, 186 n 23

Compton, 147, 157

Constantinople, 19; Chrysotriclinion 31, 32; St Sophia, 191 n 35

Coombes, 12

Corbie, 55

Corebridge, 49, 50, 66, 68, 85, 96, 109, 139, 157

Corhampton, 117

Corinth, early cusping, 126

Corringham [Essex], 145, 158

Corringham [Lincs], 143, 158

Cremona [Italy], 128

Cresiphon [Persia] palace, arcading, early cusping, twin collonettes, 125, 126

Cuixa, St Michael, 124

Cuxwold, 143, 158

Daglingworth, 62

Damascus, Great Mosque, 191 n 43

Dană [Syria], 113

Debenham, 145, 158

Deerhurst, 47, 49, 51, 91, 92, 93, 94, 109, 112, 114, 115, 117, 118, 119, 120, 122, 141, 159, 190 n 7, 54, 108

Diddlebury, 61

Dijon, St Benigne, 26, 39, 124

Dobrudja, 126

Dover, St Mary in Castro, 47, 94, 110, 120, 143, 159

Dunham Magna, axial tower, 47, 60, 61, 110, 119, 120, 145, 160

Durham, Saxon cath, 25, 46, 104

Earls Barton, 41, 43, 45, 57, 58, 87, 94, 96, 103, 109, 114, 116, 117, 119, 123, 124, 141, 160, 90

Easebourne, 12

Eastdean, turriform ch, 45, 46, 147, 161

East Lexham, 73, 76, 96, 97, 100, 104, 106, 145, 161

East Teignmouth, 82, 83, 147

Egypt, the Thebaid, *see* General and Architectural Index

El-Bagavat, funerary chapels, paintings, 131

Elmham, North, cath, 26, 60, 61, 63, 76, 145, 173

Elmham, South, Old Minster, 61, 62, 109, 145, 177
Ely, cath, 16
Ereruk' [Armenia], 26, 132
Eridu, temple with pilasters, 126
Etchmiadzin (Vagarshapat) cathedral, 29, 131, 186 n 2; council at, 186 n 2; S Gayané, ch, 187 n 12; St Hrip'simé, ch 186 n 2 187 n 12
Ethiopia, 128
Exeter, seal, 57

Feruzabad, blind arcading, 126
Fingest, turriform ch, 46
Flixton, 102
Fulda, monastery, 26, 34, 186 n 23

Galicia [Spain], 130
Gaul, 19, 20, 30
Gawrah, temple with pilasters, 126
Georgia, 126
Geddington, 117, 118
Germigny-des-Prés, centrally planned ch, 31, 32, 33, 34, 37, 38, 186 n 8, 187 n 10
Gernrode, St Cyrianus, *lisenen*, 117, 124
Gissing, 145, 161
Glastonbury, abbey, 24, 25, 82
Glendalough, St Kevin, and Trinity churches, 78, 17
Glentworth, 97, 106, 109, 112, 143, 161
Godalming, 111
Great Hale, 59, 64, 65, 85, 88, 111, 143, 162
Greatham, 100, 101
Great Ryburgh, 74
Great Tey, 47, 48, 145, 162
Guestling, 65, 66, 162
Guestwick, 61, 145, 162
Guildford, St Mary, 116, 147, 163

Haddiscoe, 73, 76, 94, 97, 119, 145, 163, 53, 71, 107
Haddiscoe Thorpe, 145, 163
Hadstock, 48
Hainton, 88, 143, 164
Hambledon, 117
Hardham, 12

Harmston, 143
Harpswell, 164
Hauran, altar with early cusping, 126
Haverfordwest, 86
Headbourne Worthy, 117
Heapham, 143, 164
Hereford, bishop's palace chapel, 38, 141
Herringfleet, 73, 145, 164
Hexham, priory, 63, 99, 186 n 7; St Mary, 30, 31, 37, 63
Hinton Ampnor, 117
Holton-le-Clay, 143, 164
Hooton Pagnall, 61
Hornby, 139, 165
Hough-on-the-Hill, 59, 64, 94, 111, 165
Housesteads, on Roman Wall, 99
Hovingham, 97, 104, 139, 165
Howe, 145, 166

Ingram, 85, 106, 166
Isle of Man, 79

Jarrow, 31, 49, 50, 67, 94, 96, 99, 102, 104, 109, 139, 166, 35
Jerusalem, dome of the Rock mosaics,, 33, 191 n 43; Kingdom of, 128
Jevington, 12, 147, 167
Jumièges, St Pierre, 99, 101

Kalb Lauzeh [Syria], 26
Kingsdown, 49
Kingston Buci, 61
Kirkdale, 102, 117
Kirk Hammerton, 88, 96, 102, 104, 109, 119, 120, 139, 167, 190 n 6
Kodja Kalessi [Cilicia], 19

Laach, St Maria Abbey ch, 124
Lambay Island [Dublin], 78
Langford, 58, 61, 94, 97, 110, 112, 116, 120, 121, 141, 167
Lavendon, 85, 94, 97, 106, 141, 168
Ledsham, 49, 51, 109, 119, 139, 168
Lérins, monastery, 19, 20, 120

Lewes, 13, 70
Lichfield, 93
Limpley Stoke, 113, 147
Lincoln, cath, 15; St Mary-le-Wigford ch, 58, 94, 97, 102, 109, 143, 169, 190 n 6; St Peter-at-Gowts, 58, 94, 97, 109, 112, 143, 169, 190 n 6, 72
Lindisfarne, 29
Little Bardfield, 87, 112, 145, 169, 135
Little Bytham, 143, 170
Little Samborne, 117
Little Saxham, 73
Little Snoring, 49
Luxeuil [France] monastery, 79
Lyminster, 12

Malles, S Benedetto, 33
Malmesbury, abbey, 82
Manzikert, battle, 128
Market Overton, 41, 141, 170
Marseilles, St Victor Abbey, 19
Marton, 58, 94, 96, 106, 112, 143, 170
Mastara [Armenia] vine scroll ornament, 191 n 43
Medeshamstede, *see* Peterborough
Middleton-by-Pickering, 94, 97, 109, 119, 139, 171
Milan, 103; S Lorenzo, 19, 25, 63, 65; S Satiro, 33, 34; S Simpliciano, 123; S Vincento in Prato, 124
Monk Fryston, 85, 95, 96, 106, 139, 171
Monkwearmouth, 30, 41, 49, 50, 67, 85, 92, 96, 100, 104, 105, 110, 114, 118, 119, 139, 171, 54, 108
Montbron, cusping, 125
Monte Cassino, monastery, 23
Montserrat [Spain] Sta Cecilia, 124
Morland, 85, 88, 106, 139, 172
Mren [Armenia] cath, figural sculpture, 131, 132
Mshattā [Jordan] vine scroll ornament, 114, 191 n 43
Münster [Grisons, Switzerland] ch, 33
Mycenae, treasury of Atreus, 80

Narberth, 86

Netheravon, 68, 109, 114, 120, 122, 147, 171
Nettleton, 59, 94, 109, 143, 172
Newhaven, 10, 61
Newton-by-Castle Acre, 61, 97, 109, 145
Northchurch, 61, 62
North Leigh, 61, 88, 96, 141, 173
North Walsham, 61
Norton, 40, 47, 94, 97, 110, 139, 173
Norwich, St Mary-at-Coslany, 145, 173, 72

Old Shoreham, 147, 174
Oshki [Georgia], 191 n 34
Ovingham, 85, 94, 96, 97, 100, 101, 104, 105, 106, 110, 119, 139, 174
Oxford, St Michael's ch, 58, 97, 101, 104, 105, 109, 114, 115, 116, 141, 174, 136

Paris, St Denis, abbey ch, 19, 20, 27, 34
Pavia [Italy] sculpture, 128
Perigueux [France] St Front ch, 27
Persia, *see* General and Architectural Index
Peterborough, cath, 46, 119; Saxon abbey [Medeshamstede], 46, 141, 175
Pomposa [Italy], 124
Provence, 19, 20
Ptghavank' [Armenia], church, 125, 131, 132
Purbeck, quarries, 45

Qusayr 'Amra [Jordan], 114

Ramsey [Hunts] abbey, 25, 46
Ravenna, chair of bp Maximian, 131; mausoleum of Galla Placidia, 123; Orthodox baptistery, 123; S Apollonare in Classe, 23, 24, 26, 103; S Apollonare Nuove, 23, 24, 185 n 13; S Giovanni, 23; S Pier Maggiore, 23; S Vitale, 23, 25, 26, 31, 37, 63, 66, 186 n 23
Repton, 47, 93, 94, 117, 118, 120, 122, 141, 175

Restenneth [Scotland] abbey, 47, 48
Ripoll [Spain] Sta Maria, 124
Rockland, All Saints, 41
Rome, Sta Costanza, 19, 25, 30, 63; Sta Maria in Capella, 24; S Paolo alle Tre Fontana, cusping, 126; Sta Pudenziana, 103; S Stefano Rotunda, 19, 30
Rothwell, 58, 59, 96, 109, 143, 175
Rottingdean, 118
Roughton, 73, 74, 76, 94, 97, 106, 110, 145, 175; 53
Ruthwell, cross, 130

St Denis, *see* Paris
St Gall, abbey, 26, 79, 93
S Germano, Sta Maria delle Cinque Tori, 33
St Riquier, 20, 21, 22, 24, 25, 34, 57, 63, 76, 79, 93, 188 n 10
Salonica, St George, 25, 63, 65
Samtavisi [Georgia], 191 n 34
Scartho, 94, 96, 102, 176
Selham, 120, 121
Sherborne, abbey, 47
Singleton, 12, 87, 94, 97, 106, 147, 176
Skellig Michael [Sceilg Mhichil], 129
Skipwith, 85, 92, 94, 95, 98, 106, 120, 139, 176; 18, 36
Sompting, 12, 58, 60, 61, 85, 88, 94, 97, 102, 104, 106, 116, 118, 120, 121, 125, 147, 177, 71, 134
Southease, 147, 177
Springthorpe, 59, 104, 178, 190 n 6
Stanton Lacy, 47, 117, 119, 141, 178
Steeple Bumpstead, 145, 178
Stevington, 141, 178
Stoughton, 12, 49, 120, 121, 122
Stow [Lincs], 40, 47, 64, 65, 110, 111, 113, 120, 179, 71
Stowe-nine-Churches, 58, 109, 116, 120, 141, 179
Sullington, 55
Sumer, pilasters on temples, 126
Swallow, 179
Swanscombe, 147, 179
Swyncombe, 60, 61
Syston, 59, 85, 96, 106, 139, 180

Talin [Armenia] cath, 125, 131
Taq-i-Bostan [Persia] arcading, 125
Tarasa [Spain] baptistery, 187 n 10, St Miguel 187 n 10
Tel Uquair [Mesopotamia] temple with pilasters, 126
Thebaid [Egypt], 20
Thetford, See of, 63
Thurlby, 59, 87, 94, 106, 180
Titchfield, 55, 147, 180
Tollesbury, 60, 61, 145, 181
Tourmanin [Syria], 26
Tournus [France] St Philibert, 24, 124
Tours, 19; St Martin's Abbey, 22, 63
Tredington, 91, 92, 97
Trier [Germany] cath, 26, 99, 102, 103
Tyrrhene Sea, 20

Ur [Mesopotamia], 126
Uruk [Mesopotamia] white temple pilasters, 126

Vagarshapat, *see* Etchmiadzin
Vaison [France] cath, 19
Vienne [France] St Pierre, 19

Waithe, 61, 96, 110, 181
Warblington, 68, 86, 88, 114, 147, 181
Warden, 112, 139, 181
Weaverthorpe, 65, 94, 97, 102, 106, 139, 182
Wendens Ambo, 145, 182
Westdean, 55, 62
Westhampnett, Norman tower, 49
West Mersea, 145, 182
Westminster, Norman abbey, 10
West Stoke, Norman tower, 49
Weybourne, 61, 110, 145, 183
Wharram-le-Street, 59, 94, 96, 102, 109, 112, 119, 139, 183
Whittingham, 85, 88, 139, 184
Wickham, 86, 95, 97, 98, 109, 147, 133
Winchester, 24, 57, 118, 188 n 12
Wing, 91, 101, 117, 118

Winterton, 94, 96, 97, 109
Wittering, 65, 120, 121
Witton-by-Walsham, 76, 145, 184
Woolbeding, 117
Wootton Wawen, 47, 48, 88, 110, 141
Worcester, Saxon Abbey, 34
Worlaby, 184
Worth, 43, 100, 101, 104, 117, 120, 122

Wotton, 57, 109, 147, 184

York, first stone church [cath], 29, 37; St Peter the Younger, 87, 97, 99, 119, 139, 184, 190 n 7; wooden oratory, 29, 30, 31, 32, 33

Zadar [Dalmatia], 37
Zwart'nots [Armenia], 125

General and Architectural Index

Ambulatory, 16, 32, 37, 187 n 10
Annexes, to W towers, 43–4, 61–2, 66–9; see also Narthex, Porticus
Apses, double, 38, 88; horse-shoe plan, 32–3, 187 n 10; single 46
Arcading, blind: German type 123, in Persia, 125–6, in Sumerian temples, 126; Lombard bands, 123, spread from East, 124–6; see also Cusping
Arches, see Openings
Armenia, influence on Western culture, 33–4, 125, 127–32; history, 127–8; earliest Christian state, 128
Art, Hiberno-Saxon or Anglo-Irish, 81, 189 n 16; see also Ornament
Axial towers, see Bell towers

Balusters, see Openings
Baptisteries, 19, 187 n 10
Belfries, 95; openings in: double, 95–7, 102, single, 97–8; lintels: flat, 96, single-arched, 96, double-arched, 96, gabled, 97, 107; genuine arches: crude, 96–7, voussoired, 97, recessed Norman type, 97, 102; see also Openings
Bell towers, 22–5, 49–60; twin western, 20, 24; early bell turrets, 22; early bell towers: 22–3, 55, spread W, 22–4; types: square, 23, circular [campanili], 23, free-standing, 23, 77, attached W, 78, lateral, 24, 49, in axial relationship, 25, 159, axial, 47, 59–61; dimensions, 47–8, 76, 86–8; porch towers, 48–56; de novo towers, 56; English Carolingian: 56–8, with pilaster strip work, 57–8; Lincolnshire bell towers,

58–9, 72; round towers: East Anglian, 70–6, 52, 72, Irish, free-standing, 77–82, 17, attached, 78, why round, 79, influence of folk memory on, 79–82; Irish-type towers: in Scotland, 79, in Isle of Man, 79, in England, 82–4

Campanili, see Bell towers
Capitals, corbelled-out, 102–3; dosseret or pulvino cap, 103, 125; ornamented, 104; influence of MS illumination, 105; cut from single stone with shaft, 105–6; Ionic, 125
Christianisation, Scandinavia and Denmark, 74–5
Chrysotriclinion [audience hall], 31–2
Churches, centrally-planned
(a) on circular axis: 16–22, 29–39; unity of tower and church, 15, 16; lantern, 16, 20–2; apsidal or niche-buttressed, 16, 186 n 2, 187 n 10; quatrefoil, 16; octofoil, 16; with ambulatory, 16, Greek cross plan, 16, 33; openwork spire-like type above lantern, 21–2; 188 n 10, n 12; in England: 29–35, domed, 16, 33, wooden, 29, stone, 29, York, 30, Hexham, 30, influence of York on W Europe, 31–4, bp's palace, Hereford, 38, doppelkapellen, 38;
(b) on longitudinal axis: Saxon ch, nature of, 10–11, Saxo-Norman overlap, 10, reason for survival, 11–13, superiority over Norman, 118–19; turriform ch, 15–25; Basilican ch, 19, 20, 21, 24; tower-chapels, 25;

Rotundas, 19, 25, 26, 39, 188 n 10, n 12; mausolea or tomb chapels, 19, 38, 80

Cloichtech, *see* Bell towers, round, Irish

Cochleae, 25

Collonettes, twin or double, 125

Coptic art, influence of, 129, 130, 131

Corbelling, of domed roofing, 80; of capitals, *see* Capitals

Crypts, 19

Cusping, origin, 125; in string course, 125; in Cluniac art, 125–6

Defence or fortified towers, 22; rare in England, 85–6; in Ireland, *see* Bell towers

Domes, *see* Roofing

Domesday Book, 11

Doorways, *see* Openings

Dosseret, *see* Capitals

Egypt, influence of, 20, 129, 131

Eremitism, in Egypt, 20; in Ireland, 129

Folk memory, influence on Irish culture, 79–82

Galilee, *see* Narthex

Galleries, 38

Hood mould, *see* Pilasters

Hypocausts, 99

Iwan, in Persian bldgs, 125

Kaiserhalle, 32; *see also* Towers, as habitations

Lantern tower, *see* Churches, centrally-planned

Lintels, *see* Belfries, openings in

Lisenen, *see* Pilasters

Mesopotamia, temples, influence of, 126

Milan, influence on Gaul, 19

Monasticism, in Ireland, 79; *see also* Eremitism

Mosaics, 33, 131, 191 n 43

MS illuminations, 105, 130; influence on capitals, 105–6

Narthex, 24, 32, 50, 66, 67, 124

Niche-buttressed ch, 118

Occuli, *see* Openings

Openings, horse-shoe, 33, 112–13, narrowing upwards, 112, unusual or unexplained, 94, 112, 114–15; windows, loop, 111–12, key-hole type, 111; occuli, 110–11, 19, 90, splaying, 111; belfry openings, columns and shafts in, 98–104, 18; balusters, mid-wall, bulging, 99, 36, 54, 72, plain, 100, banded, 100, 101, 54, 91, 107, early N type, straight, many banded, 103–4, 54, later, crudely banded [axed], 103, 90; openings in ground floor, 106–10, in one wall, 106, in two, three or four walls, 109; arches in central towers, 110

Ornament, Jews harp, 113; on standing crosses, 130–1, 191 n 43; on bp Maximian's chair, 131; soffit rolls, 120–3, 71; *see also* Cusping, Art, Armenia, MS illumination

Persia, influence on East and West, 125, 127

Pilasters, on towers, 37, 57–8, 116–18, 35, 36, 89, 90, on apses, 117, decorative or functional, 117, *lisenen*, 117; influence of Sumerian temples, 126, of Armenia, 130–1; strip work round openings, 119–20, 18, 71; hood moulds, 119

Provence, influence on NW Europe, 19

Pylons, 20, 26–7

Quincunx, *see* Churches, centrally-planned

Quoining, 39, 43, 36; *see also* Bell towers, East Anglian

Rhineland, *see* Pilasters, Roofing

Roofing, domical construction, 79–81; domes; 16, conical in Ireland, 77, in England, 82–4, Rhenish helm type, 102

Soffit rolls, *see* Ornament
Staircase towers, 23, 25–6, 52, 63–6, 89
Staircases, 25
String course, 59, ornamented, *see* Cusping
Sumer, possible influence of, 126; *see also* under Arcading

Thegn church, 13, 94
Tholoi, 80

Towers, origin, 16–19; types, *see* Churches, Bell towers, Belfries, Defence or fortified towers, Staircase towers, Pylons; flanking apses, 20–1; twin W towers, 20, 24, 188 n 8; staged and open arcaded, 21, 24; unusual uses, 88, as habitations, 91–3, 54, 108, *see also* Kaiserhalle; as W apse, 88–91; with galleries, 91–2, with altars and/or chapels, 52, 93, recesses in 88–9, 92

Vaulting, 85; *see also* Defence towers
Visigothic influence, 33, 187 n 10

Windows, *see* Openings